BRAVE QUEST

THE JOURNEY OF

INTO MANHOOD

BRAVE QUEST

A BOY'S INTERACTIVE JOURNEY INTO MANHOOD

DEAN BRIGGS

Chosen

a division of Baker Publishing Group
Minneapolis, Minnesota

Published by Chosen Books
11400 Hampshire Avenue South
Minneapolis, Minnesota 55438
www.chosenbooks.com

Chosen Books is a division of
Baker Publishing Group, Grand Rapids, Michigan

Printed in the United States of America

ISBN 978-0-8007-6275-9 (paper)
ISBN 978-1-4934-3872-3 (ebook)
ISBN 978-0-8007-6288-9 (casebound)

All Scripture quotations, unless otherwise indicated, are taken from the (NASB®) New American Standard Bible®, Copyright © 1960, 1971, 1977, 1995 by The Lockman Foundation. Used by permission. All rights reserved. www.lockman.org

Scripture quotations marked ESV are from The Holy Bible, English Standard Version® (ESV®), copyright © 2001 by Crossway, a publishing ministry of Good News Publishers. Used by permission. All rights reserved. ESV Text Edition: 2016

Scripture quotations marked KJV are from the King James Version of the Bible.

Scripture quotations marked THE MESSAGE are taken from *THE MESSAGE*, copyright © 1993, 2002, 2018 by Eugene H. Peterson. Used by permission of NavPress. All rights reserved. Represented by Tyndale House Publishers, Inc.

Scripture quotations marked NIV are from THE HOLY BIBLE, NEW INTERNATIONAL VERSION®, NIV® Copyright © 1973, 1978, 1984, 2011 by Biblica, Inc.® Used by permission. All rights reserved worldwide.

Scripture quotations marked NKJV are from the New King James Version®. Copyright © 1982 by Thomas Nelson. Used by permission. All rights reserved.

Scripture quotations marked NLT are taken from the Holy Bible, New Living Translation, copyright © 1996, 2004, 2015 by Tyndale House Foundation. Used by permission of Tyndale House Publishers, Inc., Carol Stream, Illinois 60188. All rights reserved.

For the Scripture passage quoted in Day 10, see Proverbs 5:1–8.

Scripture passage quoted in Day 14 is Proverbs 3:5–6.

Scripture passages quoted in Day 42 are Matthew 16:26, Luke 12:15, and Micah 6:8.

Scripture passages quoted in Day 46 are Luke 11:2 KJV and Zechariah 4:6 ESV.

Scripture passages quoted in Day 47 are Isaiah 30:21 and Joshua 1:7.

Scripture passages quoted in Day 48 are Psalm 26:1 and 2 Corinthians 4:2 NIV.

Cover design by Kirk DouPonce, DogEared Design

Baker Publishing Group publications use paper produced from sustainable forestry practices and post-consumer waste whenever possible.

22 23 24 25 26 27 28   7 6 5 4 3 2 1

Dedicated to my seven sons,
the true authors of this book.

CONTENTS

A NOTE TO THE FATHER, GUARDIAN, OR MENTOR

It's often said that there is a boy in every man. The older I get, the more I understand this. As a father to seven adult sons, I am also convinced of the reverse: *There is a man in every boy.* Though we tend to view the difference as a natural function of time, this is only partially true. Far better that the man in the boy be called forth.

Dad, who is your son?

Let me state here, for the record, that *stepdads are also every bit the father their sons need.* I have four biological sons and three stepsons. I invested my heart and love equally in all of them in this process—they are all my sons. Older men can also have spiritual sons they mentor, and their influence can be just as powerful as that of a biological father.

So ponder this again: Who is your son? For just a moment, don't picture the acorn of his young life. Instead, envision the oak tree. See your son as a faithful husband. See him as a father or (gulp!) a grandfather someday. Even now, he is a president, an astronaut, a doctor, a writer, a missionary, an athlete—waiting for his moment. He is a force for good in the world. It's all there, waiting for you to recognize, cultivate, extract, and affirm. Before he becomes a man, you must see that he *is* a man, longing to become.

The *Brave Quest* book you hold is only one part of a full Brave Quest Rite of Passage I recommend for maximum impact. Don't worry, I'll spell it out, covering all aspects of planning this defining moment in your son's life. The main point is this: Don't get caught flat-footed as your son comes of age. To make this experience as rich and impactful as possible, I have included a short, informative Father's Field Manual on my website, deanbriggs.com. If you are a sports fan, you may prefer to think of it as a playbook.

Regardless, after purchasing *Brave Quest* for your son (the book you now hold in your hands), you will need to get to work. Fathering is a contact sport. Don't pass it off to your wife, a pastor, or another person, and don't treat it lightly. Invest in it with prayer. Invest emotion, love, and extra time. Don't skimp—go overboard. Otherwise, you're missing the point. While the various components are important, they are *only as important as your son perceives them to be to you.* He has to see you deeply involved, encouraging him on. In that light, don't use money as an excuse. A meaningful coming-of-age doesn't have to cost a lot of money, and even the most expensive celebration can be made cheap if your heart isn't in it. If you don't have an extravagant wallet, at least have an extravagant spirit. Let your son see your excitement, as *your words and actions communicate value to him far more than money ever could.*

You are in the driver's seat, but I'm here to help. Go download the free Father's Field Manual. It will be your reference guide, while your son has the book. Though *Brave Quest* is an important part of the process, I encourage you *not* to make it the centerpiece. The centerpiece is your engagement with your son. With simple, direct guidance, I'll help you plan and execute a dynamic rite-of-passage experience that includes fifty days of story-based adventure for your son (*Brave Quest*) as preparation for a dynamic, memory-making My Dad and Me Adventure Getaway, finally concluding with the truly impacting Gathering of Men Ceremony.

Don't worry, it's not long and includes many help tools, such as timelines, suggestions, sample itineraries and activities, downloadable assets that you can customize, et cetera. I'm going to equip you with the right perspective and necessary tools to usher your son into manhood.

Just remember, you have a brief, intense window to "mancraft" your son. You will

1. summon him,
2. prepare him, and
3. commission him.

The dark days ahead will require strong men of character and confidence. If God has given you a son, it means He has entrusted you with the next generation of leadership. What a privilege! Let's make the most of it.

Visit DEANBRIGGS.COM AND DOWNLOAD FOR FREE
THE FATHER'S FIELD MANUAL.

A Note to the Young Man

You *matter.* You are important. Your life is a gift.

Many years ago, I wrote *Brave Quest* with a simple goal: to help each of my seven sons make the journey from boyhood to manhood knowing (1) how much I love each of them, (2) how much God loves each of them, and (3) how good and special it was that God made each of them a boy.

Now it's your turn.

That's why I wrote *Brave Quest* as an adventure journal, because I didn't want it to be my story; I wanted it to be *theirs*. Likewise, now it can be *yours*. As you'll see, *Brave Quest* is written from your perspective and includes space for your thoughts. Over the course of fifty days, you will literally write your own first novel (so be sure to sign your name on the first page inside the front cover)!

The best scenario is that your dad, stepdad, or male mentor handed you this book. If so, you are very likely between the ages of twelve and sixteen. Sadly, many fathers are not in their children's lives. Some have passed away; some have walked away. Let me assure you that *God has not walked away*. He wants to help father you. So if you have received this book from a special male friend or mentor who is not your dad, it is because God is working through him to fill that gap. He sees your great potential and wants to invest in your life! He wants to help make you strong in your character and confident in your purpose. Let him help you. Receive from him. Regardless of who is guiding you, throw yourself into it. Join the fun!

Remember, this book is meant to be *the adventure of YOUR life.*

So while your dad will probably have more guidance, if for some reason you are receiving this book without any other instruction, I suggest you start reading fifty days before your next birthday. Look at your birthday on the calendar, back up fifty days, and start Day 1 on that day. Each short chapter (two to three pages) will represent *one day* through the challenges of your teenage life, helping to mold you and prepare you on this most important journey of manhood. You don't have to be a victim in life. You are not fated to a small, meaningless existence. This book can help you decide who you want to be so that you can *become that man.*

Commit to a chapter a day, and take it seriously. Don't read ahead; don't lag behind. As you read and respond to the journal prompts, ask God to prepare you for a special birthday. Of course, every family is different, so birthdays may be a big deal in your family, or they may feel hidden and small. Either way, trust me: This process is a HUGE deal to God, so He'll celebrate with you no matter what. If you set aside this time in your heart, I truly believe God will mark you and set you apart in a special way for His purpose in the days ahead. You will not only experience a birthday, but you will have a summoning. You may feel it, you may dream it, or you may just know it, but I am asking God to make that day special for you whether or not it seems like anything remarkable happens. Sometimes the best things are the invisible things. At the end of the day, God is the best father. He will see. He will know. He will remember. That's my prayer for you.

One last thing: Don't be afraid. It's going to be good. This is your life. Let's celebrate.

THE
WAYPOINT

DAY ONE

THUNDER CRACKLES AND ROLLS in the sky overhead. Swirling blue mist covers your vision, rising from the loamy earth before you. Though you don't know why, you sense the fog is enchanted. On the back of your neck, hairs tingle.

"Where am I?" a voice whispers. It takes a moment before you realize the voice is your own. Realizing you are totally alone, you start to panic. Then, raining softly down from the black sky overhead, you hear something. Music. Immediately, you are filled with longing. You look around. Nothing is familiar.

You don't know where you are. You've never been here before. The music, however, is mystical and stirring. It almost feels familiar, like a memory. You cannot help but yearn for it.

Winds blow, clearing the fog. Shapes move. Light and dark and colors shift in and out.

You think, *Am I dreaming?*

All you know to do is to start walking, one step at a time. But in which direction? As the dawning light yields greater clarity, you are presented with two choices. To the left is a lush path, smoothly paved, green and living and inviting. You hear birdsongs along this path and see small animals scampering happily through the trees.

The path to the right quickly turns to broken rock and uneven land. Fallen trees and huge boulders block the path. It looks dangerous. You glance at both again. One looks comfortable and inviting. The other looks rough and uncertain. You glance left again, noticing many footprints on that path. It is well-worn, and you can see for miles. You see no footprints at all on the more difficult path to the right.

Both paths stir intense feelings in you, yet you are clearly drawn to one path more than the other. The reason is that . . .

....

....

....

....

....

....

Before you can take a single step, you hear a noise. Suddenly, a man stands before you. He wears a robe of many colors and a cloak of black. His face is thickly bearded, and his eyes burn into yours. He is fierce and terrifying: tall, but not gigantic; muscled, but not beastly. A giant sword hangs at his back. You cannot run.

"Who . . . who are you?" you ask through trembling lips.

The fierce face breaks into laughter.

"I am True Man!" he roars in a deep, rumbling voice.

"So . . . did you bring me here?" you ask, surprising yourself that you would even think such a thing. It seems strangely possible, yet how could this man have summoned you? The two of you have never met. Besides, you don't even know where "here" is.

True Man's answer surprises you.

"Of course I brought you here. But not when you think. Not now. Not this moment."

You are confused. "When, then?"

"When I caused you to be born male, this very day was prepared for you. The day of your thirteenth birthday."

For some reason, a surge of excitement shoots through your being at his words.

"LET US MAKE MAN."

GENESIS 1:26 ESV

DAY TWO

YOU GLANCE AROUND SHEEPISHLY, sure a camera is lurking nearby somewhere, filming the whole scene for some new reality TV show. Everybody is going to get a laugh at your expense. But there are no cameras. Then you realize, *He's serious.* True Man brought you here?

Okay, where is here? And who is True Man?

You are afraid. This is too weird.

True Man says, "Very often, something that is strong and strange causes others to be afraid. Does this make sense to you?"

You shrug, trying to act cool, unaffected, but True Man is an imposing figure. He does not yield. Bending down, he grips your shoulders firmly. You can feel the raw power in his hands. "Strength is part of manhood," he says gravely. "Don't ever forget that. Others may be afraid of your strength, as you are of mine. They may misunderstand you. Yes, you must be *humble* and *gentle*, but you must never be other than a man, and the first gift given to man is *strength*. This is a riddle. How do you solve it? How can you be both strong and gentle?"

....

....

....

....

....

True Man studies you in silence for several moments, then seems to accept your answer. Sensing he has more to add, you ask, "Why did you bring me here?"

"Isn't it obvious? Because you are meant to be like *me*. You have lived the life of a boy. Now it is time to begin living life as a man. Thus, I dub thee Questor. The quest of your life, since your birth as a male, has brought you to these fifty days. Be sober minded. Enjoy your journey, but do not treat it lightly. A child jokes about everything. A child cannot be trusted with deep things. By contrast, a man laughs hard and often, but also knows when to be quiet and think. Are you ready?"

"I am."

"Good. Your father will walk this road with you in real life. I will walk it with you in your dreams."

Ahh, my dreams, you realize. *That's right. I'm dreaming.*

"Almost nothing in your life will compare in importance to this, your quest for manhood. So think deeply when asked a question."

True Man hands you a faded, leatherbound book. You take and open it, surprised to realize it is, in fact, the book you already hold in your hands. It is a journal for your thoughts, but it is more. It is your life. "Nothing that will transpire over the next fifty days will be an accident. I have questions for you, but you must *be honest with yourself and me.* Answer carefully and privately. No one else needs to read what you write. This is for you and you alone, so you have no one to impress with false answers. Falsehood leads to regret. Remember, I am the *True* Man. I know your story, but this is the time for you to begin to write it for yourself."

As he speaks, he steps nearer. A part of you wishes you could run, but you feel rooted to the ground, transfixed. Only inches away, you can feel True Man's breath on your face. He doesn't move, just studies you. In his searching eyes, you see something wild and untamed, yet perfectly at peace. As if caught between that wildness and peace, you feel yourself being measured.

"Who are you?" he asks.

You start to answer flippantly—make a nervous joke—but quickly realize he is asking one of those deeper questions. One that requires more thought.

Who am I?

After a few more moments, you realize the answer is not so much what you *should* say, as if you were trying to get a good grade in school or win friends or impress your parents. Instead, he is asking for an answer only you can give, because it concerns no one but you. Seeing no judgment in his eyes, you feel released to tell the truth about yourself, the way you really feel, the good and the bad. You say . . .

....

....

....

....

....

....

....

"Well said, though I think there is more to you than you know," says the strange man. "But all in time." He pauses thoughtfully. "You have told me who you are. Your answer has been shaped by every year of your life up to now. Each of those years, you've been a boy . . . and being a boy is a very good thing! Look behind you. See that road?"

You turn, surprised to see a long road stretching behind you. You hadn't noticed it before.

"That is the Road of Youth. It has been your road. It is your past, filled with the happy memories of your life."

You look closer, surprised to see many things you recognize. Happy memories. Fun times. Blessings. A flood of gratefulness washes over you as you recognize gifts and care and love and treasures you might have taken for granted. There are hard times too. You recognize sadness, struggle, pain. But for whatever reason, looking back now, the bright moments are the ones that stand out, that make you proud and thankful, like . . .

I PRESS ON TOWARD THE GOAL.

PHILIPPIANS 3:14 ESV

DAY THREE

TRUE MAN'S VOICE interrupts your reverie.

"Every new journey is best begun with gratitude. Not everything in your past has been easy or good or to your liking. But bitterness is a poor substitute for strength in a man. Always count your blessings. If you understand this, tell me why it is true."

....

....

....

"Good," says True Man. "You stand at the juncture of manhood—a choice between two paths. This place is the Waypoint. The privileges, safety, and comforts of being a child lie behind. The joys and burdens of manhood lie before. Since every juncture requires clarity, you must know where you stand. Declare to me what you believe."

"Believe?" you say. "About what?"

"About your life. Listen to me carefully. I know the plans I have for you: *You are meant for greatness.* I choose this for you. On your journey, you will be sorely tested to hold this truth firmly in your heart. Nonetheless, I speak truth to you now. Do you believe me?"

"I guess so." You shrug, unsure what he is even talking about. "It's all this journey stuff I don't get. I'm just a kid."

True Man's wild eyes focus hard on you. "Have you been listening to nothing I've said? You are becoming a man. *Every* son of Abraham is on a journey. And every journey starts with faith. If you move from this spot without first knowing what you believe, you will simply wander, and it will be years before we meet again. Years of false manhood. Wasted time. Wasted life. You must settle what is true, what you will not yield, now. Why? Because the only thing a man will fight for is what he believes. I have made you for the battle, my son. Truth is the noble heart of every man's quest."

Interesting, you think, as True Man's challenge lingers in the air. You don't feel threatened as much as compelled. *What do I really, deeply believe about the man I am meant to become?*

....

....

....

....

....

....

Sensing your thoughts, True Man says, "Well done, that is a good start. You will find that on some things you have spoken well. Other things you will wish to add or change as your experiences become larger than your words. Time is your ally. Now you are guessing, at least in part. Later you will *know*."

He glances to the left and right, folding his arms.

"Which path do you choose on your journey to manhood? Remember, this choice is not between right and wrong. One path does not represent sin, and the other righteousness. Rather, they represent—"

"Life!" you declare triumphantly. Already, you begin to understand a little more. "The Waypoint represents the first choice a man must make: an easy life or a worthy life."

True Man seems to look at you with new appreciation and respect. His eyes widen with fierce pleasure.

"So . . . which do you choose, Questor? An easy life, or a worthy life? And why?"

....

....

....

....

....

....

....

A wind blows, and True Man's black cloak billows in the breeze. His hair catches in the wind. His eyes grow sad. "I will tell you, many men seek an easy life. Then halfway through their lives, they realize they are not really men at all. They are merely older versions of selfish little boys. They have shrunk back from challenge. They have compromised their integrity. They have looked for ease and comfort above all else and served no one but themselves. They are bored. They are aimless. This is not the path for you."

True Man points to the hard road. The right road.

"Here is where your destiny lies."

You look again at the sharp rocks, the rough road. When you turn back, True Man is gone.

THE CLIFFS
OF COWARDICE

DAY FOUR

SEVERAL HOURS OF HARD, slow progress follow. During this time, you've fallen, climbed, crawled. You've scraped your knees and cut your hands. The road is twice as hard as it looked. It is hot and dry, and you have no water. You are beginning to second-guess your decision. Worse, you are so thirsty.

After another hour, you find yourself at the base of a steep cliff. What little path you've been afforded until now dead-ends here. Sweat stings your eyes. You must either go back or up.

"Whew! Looks pretty hard to me," a voice says. You jump, startled to see beside you a thin man with a manicured goatee and coifed hair. He is dressed in fine clothes, and his skin is smooth and pale.

"Who are you?"

The man laughs, a silvery sound. "They call me Backpedaler, though I haven't the foggiest idea why. I prefer to call myself The Sage. I usually aid travelers on this road."

"Do you help them climb?" you ask.

"Heavens no!" Backpedaler throws his hands in the air. "I help them fix their mistakes and get back to *reality*."

"Reality?"

"Yes, reality. The reality that you can't possibly make this climb, and even if you could, why risk it? Can you tell me what's on top of this cliff? I, for one, have no idea. Neither do these poor folks."

He motions to the ground. There, littering the rocks, nearly blending in, you see the bleached skeletons of many dead men.

"The undecided." Backpedaler shakes his head ruefully. "I warned and warned, but they would not listen to me or take my advice. They longed to climb, yet never did. Which was *definitely* wise. But then they stayed here until they died. Don't be like them. Just go back. Just go. You can thank me later."

You hesitate, stare at your feet. There, amid the rocks and scrub brush, you notice one bony skeleton hand clutching a scrap of paper. Though it feels creepy to do so, you bend down, snatch the paper out of his fist. A few simple words are scrawled on the paper: *Multitudes, multitudes in the Valley of Decision.*

You realize you are standing in a dangerous place. It seems clear that avoiding a decision is just another form of making a decision, only far more dangerous, because . . .

DAY FIVE

YOU HEAR ANOTHER VOICE call out to you from high above. It echoes all around the canyon floor. You can't make out the words, but when you look up, you see a figure at the top of the cliff, silhouetted against the burning sun. He throws down a long rope, which drops right in front of you. The rest of the length of the rope runs up the cliff face.

"Don't listen to him, Questor!" cries the young man loudly. "Come up here. I'll help you!"

"Who are you?" you shout back.

"My name is Close Friend!" he replies. He sounds about your age. "Some call me Blood Brother. I'm here to help you go farther, higher. Just grab the rope."

"It looks too hard," you say, almost to yourself.

"*Much* too hard," Backpedaler mumbles in agreement.

"If it wasn't hard, everyone would make the climb. Don't let the Cliffs of Cowardice stop you now!"

"The reasonable man doesn't seek out unreasonable challenges," Backpedaler says cautiously.

"Columbus wasn't a reasonable man!" Close Friend shouts. "Saul of Tarsus wasn't a reasonable man! Moses wasn't a reasonable man! Alexander the Great wasn't a reasonable man! William Wallace wasn't a reasonable man! But they all did one thing reasonable men shall never do."

"What's that?" you shout back, more curious than ever.

Backpedaler starts fidgeting. "Have you seen the flowers over here? They're quite lovely this time—"

"They changed the world!" the voice from the cliff top shouts. His words echo on the canyon walls.

"Changed the world . . . changed the world . . ."

And suddenly, you know what you must do. You have made your decision. It's very simple. You tell Backpedaler, "There might be an easier way. But that doesn't make it a better way, or the right way. In fact, shortcuts often are . . .

....

....

....

....

....

....

....

You grab the rope and start to climb.

"FRIEND, MOVE UP HIGHER."

LUKE 14:10 ESV

DAY SIX

AND CLIMB, AND CLIMB. Heaving with your arms, squeezing the rope between your feet, and shoving upward.

Halfway up, your arms begin to burn with the pain of climbing. The brown rock face is streaked with blues and grays. It is hot. You are sweating, growing weak. With every pull, your arms feel like jelly. But the top is still so far away. You look down. Backpedaler is still there, waving a jug of water. You are so thirsty.

"I'm here for you, friend!" he says. "It's never too late to change your mind. And hey, don't think of it as a shortcut or copping out. It's simple: Why make it harder than it has to be? Come back and be reasonable. We'll talk."

Higher up, Close Friend calls down to you. "Focus, friend. I know it's hard. Just keep climbing. Only a little farther."

You pull. Pull again. Pull again. Your hands start to bleed.

"I can't," you say, panting. "I can't."

But you pull again anyway.

"Good!" says the encouraging voice from above.

Your grip slips. The rope burns like fire as you slide a few feet down. You squeeze so hard it feels like your skin is going to peel off. Your last few feet of progress are gone now. "I've got to go back down. I'm going to die if I fall."

When you look down, Backpedaler is a tiny figure in the faraway canyon bed. You imagine he'd be pretty friendly and welcoming and helpful if you returned. But then you think about how it would make you feel to give up. Your stomach turns at the thought. You remember a time when you gave up. You aren't proud of it. Thinking of other times when you've been tempted, you realize there are certain challenges that feel more overwhelming than others. In fact, you are most likely to give up when . . .

....

....

....

....

....

....

....

Wiping your eyes on the shoulder of your shirt, you call out, "I don't want to quit. But I don't know how to go any farther."

"Okay," says Close Friend. "Hold on tight."

You hold on. Suddenly, without doing anything, you surge upward. Close Friend is pulling the rope. You look up, but there is still a long way to go. You wonder if he is able.

"Almost there," you call out. "Keep going."

Finally, gratefully, you reach the top. Close Friend extends his hand. You take it and scramble over the edge. He is a young man with a ready smile and a mop of hair. His shirt is drenched, and he heaves for air.

"Attaboy, bro," he gasps, grinning from ear to ear. "You did great."

DAY SEVEN

"YEAH, ATTABOY!" says another young man beside him. You stare at them both. The two look exactly alike in face and form. Same height, same hair color, same eyes.

"And who are you?" you ask, pointing to the second guy.

"I'm Faker." The man grins. "I'll tell you anything to seem cool or gain respect. You'll never know the real me, but you'll think you do. And you'll like me, I guarantee it. We're bound to be the best of friends."

You smile nervously. He must be joking. "Yeah, okay."

You push aside your misgivings. After all, he seems pleasant enough, even kind of witty. Very hip and self-aware. Certainly no stranger than any of the rest of this dream. Close Friend watches you carefully, saying nothing.

"Thanks," you say, turning to look at Close Friend. "I mean, for pulling me up. I couldn't have done that last part without you."

Close Friend leaps to his feet. "Well, isn't that the way it's supposed to work?"

"How is it exactly that you are my close friend?" you ask, rising, staring at your bleeding hands. Close Friend pulls a jar out of his satchel. It's filled with a thick, jelly-like substance. You see the name on the jar. It is called *Encouragement*.

He rubs the balm on your hands, wraps them in bandages. Then he gives you a flask full of water. You drink thirstily.

"Well," he says thoughtfully, "why don't you first tell me what it is that you value most in a close friend? What are the traits and qualities you feel drawn to?"

That one is easy for you. You tell him . . .

....

....

....

....

....

....

....

"Yes, I see that about you," Close Friend says. "But dig even deeper. What makes for a rare and true friend? What is the difference between a friend and a brother? The wisdom of old tells us, 'There is a friend who sticks closer than a brother.' What do you think that means?"

As you chew on this, the answer seems clear. It means . . .

....

....

....

....

....

....

"Yes, excellent. Strive to be that kind of friend to others, for that is the kind of friend I shall be to you. Come, let's walk."

THE VALLEY
OF CURVES

DAY EIGHT

You walk together and talk, of casual things and deep things. The three of you laugh until your stomachs hurt. You pause to drink water and rest. You make up games of wit and sport. It seems as if you have known each of the other two for a long, long time.

At one point, while Faker is busy pulling apples from a nearby tree, you lean over and whisper to Close Friend, "I don't mean anything against your brother, but Faker hardly seems like a good name. I mean, he's a really cool guy. Why doesn't he change his name?"

"Oh, it's a good name for him, believe me. You just wait. But he's not my brother. There are friends, good friends, and blood brothers. And then there are fakers. You and I, we are blood brothers."

"Then why do you look so much alike?"

Close Friend stares blankly, as if the answer should be obvious.

"Because only time will tell which is which."

Just then, Faker returns. "Here, Questor. I picked the best apple for you."

Close Friend cuts him off. His voice grows firm, cautious. He is studying the land. "We are approaching the Valley of Curves," he announces. "There is much beauty here. A man can easily lose his way."

You look around and notice that you have passed from the rough ground surrounding the canyon and entered a lush region, thinly wooded and rolling with many round hills. *Curves*, you think. *Clever.* The grass is thick and soft underneath you. Wildflowers of every color dot the hillsides. Birds sing. A sparkling blue stream bubbles along, winding between the hills. *Curves everywhere.* You climb one hill after another, each more beautiful than the last. A strange sense of desire stirs in you, only growing stronger as the view of the surrounding countryside becomes more and more striking. Slowly, the sun sets, and you are left breathless at the wonder of it all. You feel strangely alive.

For some reason, the curves remind you of something. Of . . . girls. *Duh!* you chide yourself. *Curves.*

And so it is, standing on a green hill, that you admit to yourself that you have begun to notice girls in a way that seemed unappealing when you were younger. Truth be told, you kinda like them. It doesn't seem so weird anymore—no more cootie issues! Quite the opposite, your mind and body respond in unique ways, in a mix of curiosity and dread, fear and fascination.

You remember "the talk" Dad had with you not too long ago. The talk about sex. You remember Dad explaining how a man and woman fit together like two puzzle pieces. One fits inside the other—shaped that way by God, who made the puzzle of every marriage to tell a little more of His story on the earth. It is a simple fact: Girls have curves. And you've begun to notice.

Faker nudges you with his elbow. He winks. "Doesn't look so bad to me, if you know what I mean. Close Friend can be so serious sometimes. He just needs to chill."

Close Friend hears but says nothing. As if aware of your drifting thoughts, he asks, "What do you find attractive about girls, Questor?"

....

....

....

....

....

....

....

....

"Okay, that was easy. Now something harder. What confuses you about girls?"

....

....

....

....

....

....

....

....

....

....

....

....

....

....

> ## "BEWARE THAT YOU DO NOT PASS THIS PLACE."
>
> 2 KINGS 6:9 ESV

DAY NINE

IT'S STARTING TO GET DARK. You and Close Friend have had a pretty deep conversation. He nods his head in agreement about some of your observations. "Girls aren't like boys, that's for sure. But I have one more question. Before long, you will be of an age to pursue. That's a healthy, good part of manhood. But first you need to examine yourself. What do you expect from a relationship with a young lady?"

"Expect from her? Is that what you mean?"

"No, my friend. Expect from *yourself*. The man leads. It is good to contemplate and decide now: How will you lead? How will you make sure you treat her with respect and honor?"

....

....

....

....

....

....

Close Friend grabs your wrist. "In all this, you have spoken well. But be warned. You must take care in this place. The Valley of Curves *will* test your heart. Every man must pass through this land of beauty many times, so it is best you decide now how you will live in it. Decide now that your eyes will stay pure. If you will do this, your heart will follow. Grow lazy, or overly curious, and the night will take you where you do not wish to go."

Stars begin to twinkle. Over your head, the milky moon smiles a thin crescent smile. Together, you quickly set up camp.

Faker says, "You know, Questor, I've been looking for a friend like you for a long time. Man, this is great." He slaps you on the back. "I'm always going to be there for you, buddy. Just you and me."

You see Close Friend roll his eyes. He trudges off. He strikes you as very judgmental of Faker. While Close Friend is gone, you and Faker goof off and have a grand old time. By the time Close Friend returns with a pair of wild rabbits he has caught, you have decided he's just being a bit harsh. No big deal. You help gather some kindling and sticks. In short order, the three of you are happily warming your hands in front of a crackling fire, turning the meat on a spit, licking your lips with hunger, and fighting drowsiness.

After dinner, Faker pulls out a blanket and promptly goes to sleep. Close Friend unrolls two blankets from his satchel and hands you one.

"I'm wiped out," he says. "We should both get some rest. I'll see you in the morning."

He rolls over and is soon snoring. You, on the other hand, are not really sleepy at all. Dinner stirred your thoughts. In fact, you decide you would like to take a walk.

What was Close Friend getting all serious for, you think, *making such a big deal out of this place?* Just the same, you feel a sense of warning gnawing at your gut. *Turn back. Go to sleep. Close your eyes.*

You shake your head, shake the feeling away. You keep walking.

I'm just getting spooked, being silly.

As you pass beyond the fading circle of light from the fire, you notice a strange, haunting song lilting along the night air. Listening closer, you recognize a woman's voice, high and silvery, singing not too far away. The melody is almost mystical, full of magic. Almost without your realizing it, your feet begin moving.

Toward the music.

Toward her.

WISDOM SHOUTS IN THE STREET.

PROVERBS 1:20

DAY TEN

AT A CROSSROAD ALONG THE WAY, you see a woman, standing tall and firm, holding out a hand in warning. Her face is stern. Behind her and beyond a bit, the singing continues. The woman in front of you says, both warning and pleading,

> "My son, give attention to my wisdom.
> The lips of an adulteress drip honey
> Her speech is smoother than oil;
> But in the end she is bitter and sharp,
> Her feet go the way of death, and depart the path of life;
> Her ways are unstable—so keep your way far from her
> And do not go near the door of her house."

The woman does not move, does not engage you in conversation. And to be honest, you don't really want to talk to her. The singing is so beautiful, so entrancing. You leave the path at the crossroad, cutting across the grass. Before long, you approach a grove of trees. The glade is bathed in milky moonlight.

There, reclining on the grass in a sheer, flowing gown is the most beautiful woman you have ever seen. Her hair is golden, blowing lightly in the wind. Her form is voluptuous. Her fingers lightly strum a harp, and even though you do not recognize the words, your blood is stirred by the soaring enticement of her song. At first she seems unaware of your presence, and you are glad, because you secretly enjoy watching her. But then her eyes fall upon you. You feel caught. You feel ashamed. She smiles.

"Ahh, what a fine catch I've made with my song! Such a handsome young man. Do you like to listen?"

You gulp hard, nod. You cannot form a single word on your lips.

She is utterly beautiful.

She pats the ground beside her. "Come, sit. Watch me. I like to be watched."

A warning goes off in your head, like a shout. You realize that you are entering dangerous territory. The best and wisest response would be to . . .

Instead, you go and sit beside her.

"I am Miss Terry," she says coyly, batting her lashes, running a finger through her hair. Her eyelids are painted blue, her lips ruby red. She looks like a delicious piece of candy.

You fumble for words. You feel desires and emotions you do not know how to express or contain. All you can think to say is, "Please keep singing."

Miss Terry pouts. "I am tired of singing. I want to play. With you." She rolls languidly on the grass, stretching like a cat, giggling. It's obvious she's talking about sex. Her robe barely covers her body. You notice even more of her shape. You feel you should look away. Better yet, run. You never should have come. You think of Joseph with Potiphar's wife. You think of the warnings of the woman at the crossroad. You know all too well from your own life and friends that not everyone has both parents in their lives. Even so, you think of your parents' cautions.

What should you do?

THE LIPS OF A SEDUCTIVE WOMAN
ARE OH SO SWEET.

PROVERBS 5:3 THE MESSAGE

DAY ELEVEN

YOU *SHOULD* RUN. But you linger.

"I'm too young," you admit out loud, almost to yourself. "This isn't right."

"No," Miss Terry purrs. "*You* are just right. You are strong. Give me your strength."

She touches your face seductively. Her fingers run through your hair. She leans forward, close enough for you to feel her breath on your face. "You want to be a man, don't you? Isn't that why you're here?"

You've gotten plenty of advice over the years. Maybe from your mother, maybe from your father. The good advice screams in your head. Everything you've ever been trained in. All sense of right and wrong, virtue and righteousness, demands you get up, now, and leave.

Miss Terry looks at you with barely suppressed hunger coloring her eyes. She seems so exotic and forbidden. It makes her all the more tempting. "Aren't you curious what it would be like? To kiss me. To be with me."

"How do you mean, 'be with you'?"

Miss Terry smiles. "In the Bible, they call it *knowing*. After all, God made sex. Quit worrying. I've been with lots of men."

She is partially correct. God *did* make sex. So what is the big deal? How important are virginity and waiting and self-control? Do they matter, and if so, why?

....

....

....

....

....

....

....

"That's just it," you say, as you begin thinking more clearly. "Sex is meant for one man and one woman. It's meant for marriage. It's meant to be surrounded by commitment, for life. You want to pretend you are giving me something, but really you want to take something from me I can never get back."

"Oh, stop being so *serious*. Good grief. It's just sex."

"No, it's a promise I made to myself and to God."

In that moment, you realize how much you care to keep yourself for marriage, but you also realize that your own words are not entirely true, so you choose to make that promise right now. Knowing you will need God's strength, you scrawl a simple commitment:

....

....

....

....

....

....

With fresh resolve, you meet Miss Terry's gaze. "It's a gift. Not for you, but for my wife, one day, whoever she is."

Miss Terry seems taken aback at first, then mildly hurt. Then her expression becomes mischievous.

"You're playing with me, aren't you? What can be wrong with two people loving each other?"

You rise to go, feeling sorry in your heart that you ever came. You realize this has been a dangerous trap—one that you almost fell into.

"What you describe is not love. It's lust—cheap and shallow. It would not make me a man. It would only make me a fool."

You turn and stomp away.

AND SHE CAUGHT HIM.

GENESIS 39:12 KJV

DAY TWELVE

MISS TERRY CALLS AFTER YOU, PLEADING. Her eyes well with tears. "You must think I'm awful. Ugly and awful." Softly, she begins to cry.

Seeing her tears, you stop. You know you shouldn't, but you feel guilty.

Miss Terry climbs to her feet, faces you. "All I want is someone to love me. I thought that could be you. But I see now that I was wrong."

You catch a faint whiff of her perfume. It is intoxicating.

"Yes . . . you were wrong," you say, faltering.

She offers you a plain sealed envelope stuffed full of something.

"Here, take these. To remember me by."

You look at her gift. It is a manila envelope wrapped in plastic.

No! Don't touch! a silent voice screams inside. *Don't take! Run, now, run!*

But you don't run.

Off in the distance, you notice something. It is the woman from the crossroad. She is surprisingly far away, and small. You did not realize you had wandered so far from the main path. She is facing you, raising one hand palm out, as if in warning. Her voice is faint. You think she is shouting something.

"My son! Make a covenant with your eyes! Do not look upon this woman!"

You look at Miss Terry. Her eyes are warm and friendly. She seems not to have heard or noticed anything.

"Go ahead, open it. I promise you'll like what you see."

Something about the envelope compels you, attracts you. It seems forbidden and wonderful. What could be inside? How bad could it be? How good could it be? After all, you've held firm in your conviction against being with Miss Terry. You probably deserve a little gift. A reward. You glance back toward the crossroad. The other woman is gone now. Secretly, you feel relieved. She was making you feel guilty.

You open the envelope.

Photographs spill onto the ground. Photographs of Miss Terry and other women.

Naked.

Run!

You can't believe what you are seeing. They look *so* beautiful. You stare at the photos as they lie on the ground. You feel strange inside. Glancing over your shoulder, you wonder who might be watching. Your pulse races. You feel excited. Yet deep underneath, even stronger, you feel *wrong*. Through the sense of arousal, you feel like a thief—stealing what you have not been given, what you are not yet meant to know.

"Mmm," Miss Terry purrs. "You like, don't you? How do you feel right now? Be honest. What desires lie both deep in your heart and near to the surface?"

....

....

....

....

....

....

"No," you finally say. You swallow hard. A lump of lead forms in your stomach. "No!"

"Don't be silly. Take them; they're yours. You don't have to let any-one know. I'll walk away. You've already been so strong, resisting me. Just take the photos, stick them in your pocket, and it'll be our little secret. Look at how beautiful I am. This kind of sex costs you nothing. You can hold to your convictions and still enjoy all the thrills. Go on, take them."

> # BY WHAT A MAN IS OVERCOME,
> # BY THIS HE IS ENSLAVED.
>
> 2 PETER 2:19

DAY THIRTEEN

BLOOD POUNDS IN YOUR EARS. Gazing down at the photos on the ground, you feel strangely alive. Greedy, guilty, you reach down. You are no longer even hesitant. You've made your choice.

I'll just throw them away later. No big deal.

The moment your hands touch them, the photos twist and curl. Coiling like springs, they shift from paper to metal, from curls to iron chains. Like a serpent striking, they wrap around your arms, binding your wrists together.

"What?"

"'What?'" Miss Terry mocks. "'No, no, no . . . it's a promise I made to myself and to God. It's for my wife, one day . . . but I'll just take a peek today. I'll make love in my mind, but pretend I'm pure in my body.' Ha, fool!"

"What?" you repeat numbly. You strain against the chain. The forged links are unbreakable.

"Did you really think you could steal a glance and not become my slave? Don't you know? You are meant for a woman, and a woman is meant for you. There are natural, powerful forces at work in your body and soul. Urges. Hormones. The design of God. Yet not all is well. Like all men, you are a visual being. That means your eyes are doorways to your heart. Looking at a woman's naked body opens doors to places deep inside that are not yet prepared for the burdens of desire. You are becoming a man, but you are not yet. Awaken such things before you are ready, before it is safe . . . and you will be overwhelmed."

52

She laughs again. Now her beauty is terrifying. Shrinking away, you think about what she said, about awakening desires before they are ready. You realize now why this is so important. . . .

It doesn't matter. You are chained like an animal. Worse, all you can think about are the photos. All you want to do is look at more pictures. You see them in your mind. Even when you close your eyes, they are there. You can't escape.

"What are you going to do with me?" you whisper.

"What I do with all the others," says Miss Terry. "Steal your self-respect. Destroy your will. Corrupt your imagination. Ruin your marriage. I will make you small and miserable and self-loathing. Incapable of purity or honest relationships. I will fill you with shame and make you always afraid of being exposed, being found out."

She reaches down, takes your chain, and yanks it.

"Come, slave."

The Hall
of Shame

> CEASE TO HEAR INSTRUCTION,
> MY SON, AND YOU WILL STRAY FROM
> THE WORDS OF KNOWLEDGE.
>
> PROVERBS 19:27 ESV

DAY FOURTEEN

PRESENTLY, YOU FIND YOURSELF IN A LARGE ARENA, like the Colosseum of Rome, only with a vast canopy of bamboo rafters supporting a heavily thatched grass roof overhead. Giant openings in the roof and portal windows wrapping round the huge arena allow light to pour down onto the dirt floor. The enormous field in the center is made of bare earth, packed hard. Thousands of men are chained to huge stone mills, turning slow circles, grinding away the years. The hot sun bakes their skin. The walls of the arena are covered with paintings of naked women. The men stare at the pictures, many with eyes darkened by guilt, but most with simple-minded, foolish expressions, drooling. Every so often, old pictures are taken down and new pictures are hung.

"The Hall of Shame," says Miss Terry, pleased. "Every day, they grind on the Wheels of Addiction. Turning the same circles. Over and over."

You hear one man, staring in rapture at the pornography on the walls, cry out, "It's art! Such beautiful, amazing art!" But the picture he is staring at is degrading, and he is shriveled and weak. His clothes are in tatters. His hair is gray. He looks pitiful. Nothing like True Man.

"Just one more glance," another man pleads, turning another circle, looking high and low for another picture. "Just one more. Then I'll quit."

"If only my wife looked like that," announces another, to no one in particular. "*Then* I would love her. It's her fault, not mine."

You feel sick to your stomach. "How long will I be here?"

"I will own your soul probably for the next ten years. Perhaps the rest of your life. Many of these men will never be free again."

Laughing, she walks away, leaving you chained to a post, awaiting your grinding mill. You stand alone on an upper balcony, overlooking the arena floor below. You stare at the desperate men laboring below, turning endless circles. Some look foolishly elated. Most look weary to the bone. All have hollow, vacant eyes full of shame. You want nothing to do with them. Even so, you catch yourself trying to steal glances at the pictures. Angrily, you pull against your chain.

I don't deserve this, you think bitterly. *I'm not like them. I was tricked. I didn't mean to look.*

When you try to look again, your heart breaks. You realize you are lying to yourself. You *chose* to wander off the path, to pursue the singing, to reach for the photos. You wanted the forbidden. You have felt awkward with your feelings toward girls and haven't known what to do about it. You've heard your friends talk about them in inappropriate ways, and though you knew their comments were wrong, it made you curious. You never realized desire could be so dangerous.

You think of a verse you've memorized from the book of Proverbs:

Trust in the LORD with all your heart and do not lean on your own understanding. In all your ways acknowledge Him, and He will make your paths straight.

You consider the nature of desire itself. Is it *wrong*, as a boy grows into a man, to like and desire girls? What is the difference between wrong desires and right desires?

....

....

....

....

....

....

....

....

....

....

....

....

How does crooked desire lead to a crooked path? And how could "acknowledging the Lord" have kept your path straight and kept you from the Hall of Shame?

....

....

....

....

....

....

....

....

....

....

....

PROCLAIM LIBERTY TO THE CAPTIVES.

ISAIAH 61:1 ESV

DAY FIFTEEN

"PSST," whispers a voice above you.

Overhead, a section of thatched roof peels back. You see a gnarled face lean down, then the hideous, misshapen form of a hunchback dwarf. His eyes are aged and silver with sorrow. Despite the repugnance, his face is somehow tender.

"You ignored Wisdom, didn't you, lad?" he says firmly. "That woman in the middle of the road. She wasn't as pretty as you were searching for. Just passed right by her, eh? Thought she talked funny? Too stern? Ha! Wisdom, if you'll listen to her, follow her paths, get her words deep inside you—she'll save your bacon more than a time or two." The ugly hunchback shakes his head ruefully. "Didn't make sense enough for you, eh? I reckon, truth be told, you didn't much want it to make sense."

You shift uncomfortably, darting your eyes away from the dwarf and then back.

"Think about it, lad. How often do you disobey, go down your own path, do your own thing? Are you known for obedience? For submitting your will? Not just in this area, but with anything? You name it. In what areas do you fail the most?"

....

....

....

....

The dwarf continues, "So you passed Wisdom by and came to that pretty glade with that pretty lady, Sweet Seductress—"

"Miss Terry?"

"Aye, you got that right! She's all about secrets. Stolen Waters, some call her. She's a riddle beyond figurin'. Over and over, men come begging—fools thinking she'll make them a king—and she carries them away as slaves. Easy as pudding. Happens every day. Men who don't know what's good for them. Cowardly, selfish men, governed by nothing but what they feel and want. No thought of others, only themselves. No steel or self-control, no grit or humility. Lonely men."

You feel more than a little embarrassed but don't want to show it. "Who are you?" you ask, glancing up and down the balcony to see if anyone has noticed you or your visitor.

"Many things, lad. I am many things. Some never give me a thought. Others think me weak and crippled. My name is Brother Kennis." He pulls a small name card out of his tattered shirt pocket. "Here," he says, dropping it into your hands. You read, *Bro. Kennis, Repair and Restoration Expert.*

Kennis continues, "I often come secretly to this place and to many other prisons of the soul. Whenever a heart cries out for mercy, I am there. So it is, just now, that I came to you. I have come to ask you one question. Answer carefully, for the task of liberty is not for the faint of heart, and I have no time for silly games. Young man, do you want to be free?"

"Yes!" you cry. The very thought makes you drop to your knees and weep.

"Tell me, then. Write your prayer. Though your hands are bound, you can still scribble out a prayer for freedom, purity, and submission, now and in the future."

TRUTH IN THE INNERMOST.

PSALM 51:6

DAY SIXTEEN

AS YOU SUBMIT YOUR PRAYER, Brother Kennis smiles. You look up, see him scattering a powder into the air above you. Golden, it shimmers as it falls, lighting on your shoulders. You feel it on your face. You breathe it in. As you inhale, a deep sense of conviction overwhelms you.

"This, boy, this is the gift I give. It comes from True Man, who sent me to rescue you. It is called Repentance."

With brutal clarity, even as the chains bite into your skin, you feel the truth of your emotions bite into your soul, drawing blood. Angrily, you wrench at your chains, but they will not budge. And so you realize the secret motives that brought you to the glade in the first place: stubbornness, self-will, pride. You wanted it *your* way. You didn't want to listen to Close Friend's warnings. You didn't want to heed Wisdom. You wanted the Sweet Seductress, period. You wanted the photos. You wanted thrill and satisfaction.

No one else brought you to this place. You alone. Knowing this, you embrace the blame. No more excuses.

As you do, a pain stabs your heart. Shocked, you realize that before Brother Kennis came you were sorry only in part—mainly for having been caught. Now it is different. Now you are grieved that you desired what could have destroyed you. A bitter truth settles upon your heart.

Tears streaming down your face, you say, "I can't win this on my own, Brother Kennis. I will never be free unless I am *set* free. I will never be man enough to win the heavy battles of the heart. Somehow, I know that to the core of my being."

"Know what?"

You summarize. "Everyone needs salvation."

You feel defeated, not liberated. Your bonds are not made of metal, but of lies and lust. Though you gasp with sorrow, you refuse to deny it.

Kennis chuckles softly, pleased. "You have gained a valuable truth, Questor. At such a young age, it can save you a great deal of pain and heartache. The fact is, no, you cannot *ever* be good enough or strong enough. You can make good decisions, yes. You can be wise and humble. You can be honest about your weaknesses. You can obey. But ultimately, only True Man can set you free and *keep* you free. So let's pretend that very thing. Look into your future. If you could be free, how would you conduct yourself differently in the future? What different choices would you make—specifically, when faced with the temptations of lust?"

DAY SEVENTEEN

THE HUNCHBACK, still peering down from the roof, says, "This is all very good news, my boy. Confession cleanses the soul. And in every place you are weak, True Man wants to be strong. For you, in you, with you. He can break any chain."

"I wish he would break mine," you sob, full of conviction. "I wish he would break mine right now!"

"Lad, he already has. Look!"

Unbelieving, your eyes dart to your wrists. The metal chains have changed. In their place, on your wrists, a familiar envelope rests. The very same one Miss Terry gave you. You can feel the weight of the photos inside. They beckon you with promises of secret pleasure.

"Repentance," Kennis says, "is not merely sorrow. It is turning from your pride and sin and wrong ways. Freedom, on the other hand, is having the power to choose what is right. Explain this to me in another way so I know you understand."

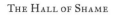

"Good," says the dwarf. "So what do you choose?"

You stare at the envelope. You could open it again. One more time, just once, you could look.

You shout your answer: "*Freedom!*"

Your voice echoes. The men below glance up fearfully, see you tearing the envelope into tiny pieces and throwing it down. They see you spit on the ground, stomp the pieces into the dirt.

The dwarf laughs. "Well said, indeed! Now, let's get out of here. Take me hand. Let's go higher."

"I don't think you're strong enough to lift me," you say hesitantly.

"So I've been told. Like I said, many think I'm ugly, weak. Now, stop talking and just give me your hand, boy. Find out for yourself."

You reach for his arm. With a mighty heave, you are swept upward. The dwarf's strength is astounding. His grip is like iron.

"Follow me!" he whispers harshly.

As you dart away across the rooftop, you hear a familiar voice. Miss Terry. Only this time, she is shouting in rage.

"Kennis! Kennis, you dog! Give me back my slave!"

You shudder. Then, into the night, you are away.

DAY EIGHTEEN

AFTER RUNNING AND CLIMBING and running and climbing—so fast and far from the Hall of Shame, your lungs are burning—you come to a wide river. On the near side, a boat is moored to the docks. Dawn is near, but the night is still dark.

"You must get on this, quickly. She will still hunt you. The Seductress does not give up easily. This vessel will take you to a place where you will be made strong."

You board quickly. The captain greets you.

"Ticket, please."

You stare at him blankly, then back at the dwarf.

"Look in your pocket," says Brother Kennis.

You shove your hand into your pocket, surprised to pull out a sales receipt. It is plain white, except for a barcode at the bottom and a serial number that reads, *J-OB-2310.*

"Excellent," says the captain. His brows arch with admiration. "This is precisely the journey we are on. My name is Destiny, if you need to know. Welcome aboard the *Sonship*. We'll travel quickly and transfer you to another boat soon enough. That's the one that'll take you where you really need to go." He slaps the ticket against the palm of his hand and winks at you. "Seems True Man has his eye on you for great things, so think about what you want to do with your life. Where do you want old Cap'n Destiny to take you?"

....

....

....

....

....

The wind is blowing, and the world feels green again. You are glad to be out of the Hall of Shame and on your way. You feel a fresh resolve to keep your feet on the straight and narrow.

"Exactly where are we going, Kennis?" you say, expecting your friend. He is not there.

The captain notices your vain search. "Brother Kennis is gone, friend. Heard the call of another soul. Down in the Valley of Drunken Sorrows, I reckon, judging from the direction he headed."

That is all the chitchat to be had. Captain Destiny barks orders at his crew, who begin scurrying about. Unmoored at last, the *Sonship* sets sail. You are exhausted and soon fall fast asleep in the hold below. You are so sleepy, in fact, that you don't even realize when the vessel docks again. And when you are shuffled to the next boat, you are almost too tired to notice the faded name of the second boat painted on its prow.

Hardship.

ADVERSE
CITY

> FOR THE MOMENT ALL DISCIPLINE
> SEEMS PAINFUL RATHER
> THAN PLEASANT.
>
> HEBREWS 12:11 ESV

DAY NINETEEN

YOU AWAKE TO THE STING of a lash across your back.

"Off my ship, ya dog!"

You yelp, flinch away. Your brain is still trapped in a thick fog, but you don't recognize the captain anymore. Reeling from confusion, you stumble forward, realizing you are marching down a gangplank. The river now tunnels underground, and the boat has lodged against a rocky embankment. You are the only one disembarking.

Blinking your bleary eyes, you find yourself in a series of dark caves. Only a handful of other men are down here. They have miners' lights and pickaxes and are scattered about, chipping rhythmically away at the rocks. They are grimy with sweat and dust. Some appear determined, others bitter. All look weary. Offhandedly, you notice something else. . . .

These guys look tough.

Indeed, all of the men are lean, hardened, and toned with muscle.

"All right! New recruit coming down the plank!" a man bellows, shoving you forward. He is a huge man in a leather jacket, bald, with brass knuckles in one hand and a black leather whip in the other. He wears a badge on his shirt. It reads, *Testing.*

"Welcome to the Underground. Known to the uplanders as Adverse City. Listen close, grunt! You won't be treated fair or friendly here. Don't expect respect or admiration. You will be belittled, mocked, and made to do hard work, alone, for no pay. You will toil in obscurity while others above succeed. You will be betrayed, forgotten, forsaken. That's pretty much the deal. Don't come to me for sympathy. No one understands, and no one cares. Just take your pickaxe and get to work."

He shoves one of the heavy tools into your hands. You are finally fully awake, enough to realize this is bad. Fear rises in your gut. As you allow your eyes to adjust to the dim light, you begin to feel the claustrophobia of the mines closing in around you. A dozen or more shafts shoot off into the darkness from the central dock, like spokes on a wheel radiating outward.

"I don't understand," you say. "What did I do to deserve this?"

"Don't know. Don't care."

"I don't know how to mine. I don't even know where to go. And I'm hungry."

Testing smacks you hard on the back of your head. "Pay attention for once in your life!" he growls. "This *isn't* a vacation. The Mines are all clearly labeled. You have Shafts of Obscurity, Delay, Resistance, Betrayal, Poverty, Punishment, Illness, Injustice. Others, too. But you, you're scheduled for . . ." He checks his chart. "Ooh, we haven't had one of these in a while."

You swallow hard. "What's it say?"

"This shaft is called Shepherd's Rod."

"What does that mean?"

"It means it is beyond our knowing." For the briefest of moments, he seems to soften. He flips through his papers, studies his clipboard. "Tell you what. I'm assigning someone to work with you. His name is Gritt." Then his face grows hard again. "Don't say I never gave you anything." He hands you a plain gray shirt. In simple block letters, the front reads, *I Got the Shaft in Adverse City.*

"Cute, huh, sweetie? Get used to it. This is your new identity. Your work shirt. Put it on and get to swinging. I'm tired of looking at you."

He bends down, clasps iron shackles around your feet, then shoves you toward Shepherd's Rod. You clench your teeth, feeling shamed and angry. Seems like you barely escaped one set of chains. Now you are in another.

As if reading your thoughts, Testing mocks you. "These chains aren't like the bondage of sin, fool. These are the Shackles of Discipline. Specially forged for those in Adverse City. Hey, just for grins, what do ya think the difference might be? Do ya think a rat fink like you can put two and two together and come up with four? Go on. I need a good laugh. What's the difference between bondage to sin and the bondage of discipline?"

You struggle to ignore the sarcasm. You *know* the difference. Or at least you think you do. . . .

YOU MEANT EVIL AGAINST ME,
BUT GOD MEANT IT FOR GOOD.

GENESIS 50:20 ESV

DAY TWENTY

YOU STUMBLE OFF INTO THE DARKNESS with no clue what you are supposed to do. You just put one foot in front of the other. The shackles keep your steps short, your stance tight. You are forced to walk a tight line, maintain balance. You fall many times, scraping your knees, bruising your elbows.

Where is Close Friend? Where is Brother Kennis? Where is True Man? Why won't anyone rescue me?

The stone walls seem to whisper back an answer you shudder to contemplate.

They don't care, that's why. They've forgotten you. You will rot here forever.

Only a few dim lanterns illuminate the rough-hewn stone. Shuffling forward, you feel the weight of your imprisonment fall upon your shoulders like a collapsing building. The earth above and around feels heavy and oppressive.

How did I get here? What did I do to deserve this?

After what seems like miles of lonely travel, stumbling for light, bleeding, you come upon a solitary figure, slowly chipping away at the rock face. He is neither young nor old.

"Hello," you say, but your voice sounds like a growl. You realize your throat is parched. "What . . . what is your name?"

"I am Future Leader 104," the man says. "I am being prepared for great things. Be patient, lad. Spend your time here well. Everyone will face difficult times on this earth. No life is spared."

You want to talk more, but the man seems quite focused on his task, so you move on. A little farther into the shaft, another man, grayer than the previous, strikes at the rock angrily, cursing under his breath.

"And you are . . . ?"

The man turns one bulging eye to stare at you. His other eye is rotted and dark. "Like it really matters," he mutters. "Probably just here to mock me like all the others. Or worse, ignore me. I keep trying to tell people, the world *owes* me! I deserve better than this. Does anyone listen? No. So go ahead, do your worst! Call me Grudge, like all the others. I had a different name once. I think it was 89. Future Leader 89, or something like that. Ha! What a fool I was to ever believe that. Don't ever dream big, kid. Hard times hit you like a hammer. Dreams die. The world will crush your soul. Now get out of here and leave me alone! You're wastin' my time."

You shuffle along, shivering. As you ponder the difference between the two men, you think about hard times you have faced. Challenges, setbacks, unfairness. How have you responded to them? How have they affected your attitude or outlook on life?

COUNT IT ALL JOY.

JAMES 1:2 ESV

DAY TWENTY-ONE

YOU ARE IN A DAZE IN THE MINES when you bump into something. Or someone. A low, rough voice responds.

"Easy, fella. Hey, chin up, now. Watch where you're going. Gonna hurt old Gritt, you are," says a man in front of you, smeared with grime and sweat. He isn't old at all. In fact, he looks rather young, perhaps twenty. A miner's light on his forehead shines in your eyes. He is muscular and wears a ready smile. "We've been assigned to work together, I think. All up and down this channel. I was startin' to wonder when you'd show up. Now here you are, and I'll tell you plain. I'm ready. I could use a friend. What do you say we tackle this area here?"

He swings his axe hard at a clump of rock streaked brown and red, barely breaks off a small chunk. Swings again. The pickaxe glances off, making a high, pinging sound. The stone is very hard. Gritt swings again and again. Finally, another chunk breaks off.

"I don't give up easy." He grins. "Besides, some of the best stuff is behind the toughest rock. I've learned not to mind these assignments."

"Why are you even here? Why am I here? This doesn't make any sense."

"Let's see: Don't know, don't know . . . and I agree. But we might as well make the most of it. You know, fight. Endure. Make lemonade out of lemons. All that stuff."

"But this is so unfair!" you cry out, very near to sobbing. The iron shackles bite into your ankles. The air stinks. You wonder if you will ever see daylight again. Why did Brother Kennis bring you here?

"Life is not *always* fair, my friend—quite the opposite. You should know that by now. The question is, how are you going to handle it?

Chin up, with courage? Or give up and quit? Blame others. Whine, pout."

"I didn't ask for this!" you shout angrily. "Not one bit!"

"Join the club. No one asks for lemons. No one asks for rain, or pain, or trouble."

You wrinkle your face in disgust. *There he goes with lemons again.*

The phrase sticks in your craw, irritates your brain. On a scale of one to ten for making lemonade out of lemons, you rate yourself in your head. You realize there is a key difference between how Gritt looks at the world and how you look at it. The difference is . . .

....

....

....

....

....

....

....

....

....

....

....

....

....

ADVERSARIES REVILE ME.

PSALM 42:10

DAY TWENTY-TWO

You don't want to talk anymore, so you start swinging your axe. Blisters quickly form on your hands. You bleed. You sweat. You soon grow weary. Hours turn into days. You are fed tasteless mush for every meal and given dirty water to drink. You sleep on cold, hard stone with no blanket. You have no idea whether it is day or night outside. You feel forgotten, numb. Where is Close Friend now, when you need him most?

The taskmaster's men pass by every now and then to check on you. They are well-dressed, clean, successful. You feel small, embarrassed to be around them.

As if sensing your insecurity, one of the guards laughs at you, pointing at your meager chippings. "Aw, is the axe too heavy for you, pookie? Get a life! My sister could break more rock than you."

His companion snickers. "Now, now, Spite. Take it easy. After all, the boy wasn't even man enough to handle Miss Terry."

"Oh, man. I forgot you told me that, Bully. What a loser! What a total loser."

"Plus, Spite and me heard you just up and left your best friend stranded out there in the woods, alone with the wolves. Probably robbed him blind first. Nothing but a thief and a coward, I'd say."

"And don't even know what to do with a pretty thing like Miss Terry? I almost take that personally. For her, I mean. Did you hurt her feelings, punk? Did you make her cry?"

He backhands you. "I hope you rot here forever, moron."

Spite grabs you, holds you while Bully punches you in the stomach. You double over, gasping for breath.

"How's that feel, Mr. Judas? Mr. Shrimp. Maybe you should learn to treat your friends better. Act like a man for once. Grow up."

They walk away, chortling. One of them shouts back, "The boys took a vote. The moment you stepped off the gangplank, we nominated you 'Most Likely to Never Matter.'"

They erupt into hoarse laughter again. Slowly, their voices fade.

You look up at Gritt. "I didn't betray anybody. You've got to believe me. They're lying."

Gritt nods. "I could try to make you feel better right now. I could tell you I believe you. But True Man taught me to go deeper, to stand alone if needed, to not be distracted by what others think of me. Just do the best you can and stay humble, Questor. If you do those two things, what anyone else thinks about you is *their* problem, not yours."

You think about this. How much do you depend on what others think of you?

....

....

....

....

....

....

....

....

....

....

....

You have need of endurance.

HEBREWS 10:36 ESV

DAY TWENTY-THREE

THE STRESS AND SWEAT and difficulty continue. Gritt labors hard beside you. One day—it seems like weeks have passed—he strikes the rock, and out falls a chunk of something that glitters.

"Ahh!" he whispers with delight. It is a large chunk of pure gold. "Now, that's a keeper."

You stare at him, stunned.

"What do you mean, 'keeper'?"

"It's what I've tried to tell you, Questor. There is nothing fair about getting shafted. There is nothing fair about barely surviving your time in Adverse City. Even so, your days or months or years do not have to be wasted. Whatever treasures you find—they are yours to keep. Forever. The taskmaster will not take them from you. No one can."

"You mean, if I find treasures here, and one day I escape this place, I could be rich?"

Gritt smiles. "Starts to change the equation, huh? Wealth far greater than money. Do you know what I'm talking about?"

....

....

....

....

"But how long will I have to work?" you ask. "Where do I find them? How long before I can go free?"

"Don't know times three. But really, you're missing the point. Just be faithful. Look hard. Keep your chin up. Find reasons to be thankful. If it was easy, everyone would want to come here."

You shake your head. "How do you know all this?"

Gritt smiles. "Nothing special about me. I've just been a pupil of True Man for many years."

You swing the axe again, this time with a bit more eagerness and a bit less resentment. Strangely, the axe feels lighter.

Days and weeks pass again. The security guards come by every so often for no good reason except to mock and tease and beat you. You hear more rumors of what the uplanders think of you. None of it is good. You feel greatly misunderstood. The constant clinking of the chains on your feet drives you nearly to insanity. Still, with Gritt, you keep swinging. Though the food is tasteless, the water is brown, and the air in the tunnels is either stiflingly hot or bitterly cold, you give yourself to the labor and learn to be thankful for simple things. Food, water, rest. You have decided that while Adverse City is no place to live, neither is it a place to quit.

"I just want to get out of the Mines!" you say one day, weary, striking at the rock with extra force.

"Yes, good," says Gritt. "'The Mines' are a dark, bottomless hole. Self-focus traps you in a small life. You are meant to be larger than yourself, but it can only come about by learning character, learning to serve others, learning to—"

"Care about others more than myself?" you say. As they flood your thoughts, you realize how many "mines" you've been trapped in.

....

....

....

....

....

Then you think of one time in particular when you served someone without being asked, without thought of reward or recognition. You did it because someone needed help. Because it was the right thing to do. You remember how it made you feel.

....

....

....

....

....

....

You didn't know it at the time, but you realize now that you felt more like a man that day.

A fresh new thought enters your mind. *It's good to feel like a man,* you think. *If I'm meant to be a man, it's good to feel like a man. I should do those things that make me feel like a man and avoid the things that don't.*

With a fresh pang of sorrow, you realize you did *not* feel like a man in the Hall of Shame. You felt like a slave. Though the desires were masculine, the use of them was corrupt.

Men are meant to be free, you think.

Hidden wealth of secret places.

ISAIAH 45:3

DAY TWENTY-FOUR

GRITT IS STARING AT YOU, a funny expression on his face. You realize that for several moments you have been lost in thought. Your axe point, biting deeply into the stone, is stuck.

"Push! Pull! You've got ahold of something," says Gritt.

Groaning, you pry the handle up with all your might. You strain all your muscles. The veins on your neck pop. Finally, a huge chunk of black rock falls, exposing a small cavity in the shaft wall. Inside you see a small golden chest.

"Whoa!" breathes your friend in a low voice. "Dude, that looks serious. Get it! What's inside?"

The box is simple—wood overlaid with gold. The lid opens easily. Inside are a note and three ancient-looking scrolls.

> *Weary traveler, you have put forth your hand upon the rock, you have spent your strength in the labor of dark and hidden places. You have submitted to the quest for character, wisdom, and humility. Find now treasures to sustain your life: Integris, Veritas, Valorium.*

"The Three Lost Scrolls," breathes Gritt, eyes wide with wonder. "The whole world has been searching for those!"

Carefully, you lift the scrolls. They tingle on your skin as if electric. The sheets are heavy, made of lambskin or something like it.

"Should I open them now?"

Gritt doesn't answer. "What's that other thing? That note there in the bottom?"

You notice a small, unadorned envelope in the bottom of the box. It is sealed, but the outside reads, *Certificate of Release. Present to taskmaster immediately.*

"Sounds like your ticket outta here," Gritt says. For some reason, he doesn't sound jealous at all. In fact, he almost seems proud.

You stare at him, afraid to believe it could be true.

"Do you really think . . ."

"Only one way to find out."

You hesitate. "Come with me."

Gritt holds up a hand, shakes his head. "No, no. My place is here. Other Questors will be along soon enough. I know you think I'm young, but I'm really six thousand years old. My first and proudest name is Perseverance of the Saints. My first visitor was your father, Adam. He'd lost his way big-time, let me tell you. True Man sent me to help him. Others will need me too. I'll be here for them, down in the darkness, when they want to give up. Like you, they will take a part of me with them wherever they go, when they are finally free." He places his hands on your shoulders. "Go with this command: *Endure.*"

"Thank you," you reply. Amazingly, it is almost hard to leave. Gritt has become a part of you. Yet surging with hope, you drop your axe. Clutching the Three Lost Scrolls and the certificate of release, you hurry away, down the long shaft toward the river at the heart of the Mines.

DAY TWENTY-FIVE

THE TASKMASTER NAMED TESTING sees you coming. Other prisoners and security guards notice you too. They rise to block your path. Some of them pick up rocks to throw, some draw swords. Others hurl words and insults. You duck your head and begin waving your certificate.

"Hold!" shouts Testing. The guards stop. You pass by. Dropping to your knees, you lower your head and present the certificate. The taskmaster takes the note, opens it, reads it aloud.

> "Hardship embraced,
> Though wronged, misplaced,
> Opportunity creates,
> Promotion awaits.
> By royal decree,
> Open the gates."

Testing stares at you. His expression is stern, unreadable. "Fine. I don't like it. But fine. The same ship that brought you shall carry you away."

You look. The vessel bobbing gently in the current of the river bears the name *Favor*.

"But *Hardship* brought me here," you protest.

"It is the *same* vessel," Testing says in a tone that does not invite challenge. "Only you have changed."

You remember another particularly difficult hardship in your life. A time not so much of painful sorrow or regret, but testing and unfairness. You remember how it changed you, for both good and bad—how you responded well and poorly. You understand more now. *If I could*, you think, *how would I handle it differently?*

....

....

....

....

....

....

....

Testing bends down, inserts a key into the lock of your foot chains. You have grown so used to walking a tight line, weighed down, you can hardly believe the lightness and range of motion you feel.

"Go now," says the taskmaster, showing his teeth in a cruel smile. "But know this. Over the course of your life, I will see you *many* more times. It is inevitable. Though it's hard and desperate, many fools come to value their time here more and more. Be wiser than they. Fear me. I'll always be waiting, ready to crush your soul, and I hate it when men no longer dread me. My fondest desire is to break you beyond recognition. Only bitterness awaits you here."

You hear him, but in truth, he seems smaller, less threatening. Besides, clutching the Lost Scrolls to your chest, you know otherwise. You leave with *treasure*, not bitterness. You climb aboard the boat, find a spot on the deck. Safe at last, you feel tears slide down your face. You have never endured such a trial as this. But you feel stronger, more determined, more ready for whatever challenges lie ahead. Somehow, there is a sweetness to the darkness of this place.

"I'm ready," you say to the captain.

Unmoored, the boat drifts into the current of the river, picks up speed. The Mines fade from view.

MEN OF VALOR IN THEIR GENERATIONS.

1 CHRONICLES 7:2

DAY TWENTY-SIX

AFTER A HALF DAY OF TRAVEL, the river terminates in a vast cavern. Here, the collected waters swirl gently in a circle with no place to go. The channel has ended. Overhead, the ceiling vaults away into an inky blackness that the lanterns of the ship cannot penetrate. A tiny pinpoint of light is all you see at the very top. It feels like it could be miles away.

Captain Destiny approaches you.

"Do you see it?"

He points. In fact, you had not seen it. Dropping down from the center of the vaulted ceiling, as if from nothing, is a thick rope attached to a large bucket. The rope trails upward into shadows, seemingly hung upon nothing. The bucket sways gently. Steering closer to the bucket, the captain urges you forward.

"Go on, get in."

"What?" you exclaim. The bucket is surely big enough for a person. But why in the world should you get in it?

"It may not look like a promotion. And I can't even tell you how it works. All I can tell you is, you've got to get out of the boat."

You don't even try to hide your exasperation. "I don't want to get out of the boat! I just want to get out of this *mountain*." Exhausted, you wipe your eyes. "Is anything ever normal around here?"

"Take a step, lad," the captain says gently. His eyes sparkle. "Have a little faith."

Angrily, you reach for the rope, climb into the bucket.

"There!" you say defiantly.

"Attaboy. But you better hold on. They tell me this can be a wild ride."

87

You never even see the captain disappear. In fact, the captain does not. You do. Without warning, the bucket shoots skyward, like a rocket launching. It moves so fast, so suddenly, the colors of your dream start to bleed together. You feel yourself shaking. You feel wind. You feel terror. One thing you cannot do, at all, is *see*. It's all happening too fast. You have become a human bullet, aimed straight up. Squatting inside the bucket, screaming, you clutch at the rope and the rough wood for dear life. Slowly, the tiny speck of light at the top begins to enlarge. You dare not look down.

As you blast upward, in the midst of the terror you feel a pure sense of joy, of thrill. You feel like a superhero. Superman or Spider-Man or the Green Lantern. Soaring. A strange thought to think at a time like this, but if you could be a Marvel or DC Comics character, you know who you would choose. You think about why. . . .

....

....

....

It occurs to you that there is a little bit of a superhero in every man's heart. You remember a cherished time when you did something brave or daring. It was risky. But you did it anyway. . . .

....

....

....

....

....

....

FROM WEAKNESS WERE MADE STRONG.

HEBREWS 11:34

DAY TWENTY-SEVEN

AS YOU TRAVEL HIGHER, you see that the light at the top is actually blue. You are staring up at the sky, looking through a hole cut in the top of the mountain. In the span of about five minutes, you've gone from the very bottom to the very top. You taste the words on your lips.

Promotion. Advancement.

The bucket starts to slow. You notice a ledge of rock that extends a few feet into the opening at the top. The bucket comes to rest level with the platform.

A familiar voice greets you.

"Welcome, Questor," says True Man. He laughs loudly and heartily. "It's good to see you."

Relief floods you as you reach for his outstretched hand. Gratefully, you climb out.

"You've come a long way," True Man says. He is wearing clothes made of thick brown grizzly fur. His voice is deep like you remember. He is just as tall, just as strong. His beard is just as heavy, his eyes just as fierce. Yet, for some reason, you no longer find him strange. Near to him, you feel safe. It has been a long time since you have felt safe.

A torrent of emotion wells up.

"Faker betrayed me, or maybe I betrayed myself," you blurt out, choking on your words. "Maybe he lied about me. I don't really know how it all happened, but I woke up in the Mines under this mountain. It's been months, I think. They made us all work so hard, night and day. They were cruel. I felt like a slave."

You want him to rage, to seize the massive broadsword slung across his back and charge down the mountain to avenge you. Instead, he turns, says one word.

"Come."

You follow him down a winding path through crunching snow.

As you walk, a pang of memory hits you.

"Whatever happened to Close Friend?" you ask.

True Man smiles. "Ah, never fear. You will see him again. He will have an odd way of being there throughout your life, though perhaps he may look different when you see him next. Besides, others need him, too."

For some reason, that satisfies you. You double your stride to keep pace. The air is mountain thin and laced with swirling streamers of fat white flakes falling from the sky. Evergreens sag under burdens of powder as fine as talc. The sun is painfully bright. The sky is pale blue. Half your field of view drops away to nothing beneath you, falling down steep cliffs, sweeping across miles of crags and jagged spikes and a fertile valley of green lost in the mist far below. You tromp perhaps a hundred paces through the woods behind True Man, who does not speak a word. Finally, you reach a clearing. A pool of dark water steams at its center.

"Look," says True Man, pointing.

You lean over the water to see what he sees. There, in the surface, like a mirror dimly, you see yourself for the first time since beginning this journey. Your shirt is torn to shreds from the labor in the Mines. You are startled to see your face and frame. Your jawline is angled and square. Your biceps and triceps are defined. Your chest and abdomen are knotted with muscle. As you look at yourself, the water ripples. Now you carry a sword made of black metal. All around you, a battle rages. You gasp at the determination you see in your own face. With your eyes alight, you charge into the ranks of an unseen terror. An entire army rallies to your cry. . . .

"Now look at your hands."

You obey, flexing your fingers in front of your face.

"Those are a man's hands. Not a boy's. They are meant for a sword, for battle. Now look again. What you first saw is true. Reflected now in the water, behold another image of yourself, of what you would look like in the future if you had not endured Adverse City."

Once more, you lean over the water. You see a version of yourself you easily recognize. Your face is smooth. Your body is little changed. Your eyes are soft and dreamy. In this vision, a similar battle rages. You see the world collapsing all around. Desperate people cry out for help. But you give none. Your eyes are timid and fearful. You cower. Your arms have no strength. You carry no weapon. In the vision, you can feel yourself wishing it would all just go away.

You shudder at the sight, close your eyes, ashamed.

"I was a fool with Miss Terry. I should have listened to Wisdom."

"The Mines are difficult," True Man says solemnly. "But slavery is a greater torment by far. Every great man sails the *Hardship*, or he is not made great. And every great man will fall because none are true but me. What makes them great is to keep moving forward, humbled, and therefore always ready for my aid. Looking back, whipping yourself with guilt and wasting time wishing you could change the past will only make you ripe for another failure. You may not know it, but it is true. Tell me, why do you suppose this is?"

MOUNT
TRANSFORMATION

DAY TWENTY-EIGHT

RISING FROM WHERE YOU KNEEL beside the pool, you face True Man.

"I have grown strong," you admit. "But I have no sword."

"Time enough for swords. First you must know who you are. Only then can you defeat foes greater than yourself. You must fight to *be true* before you can fight *for* truth. If you do not fight with what you have in here"—he pushes hard against your chest—"and here"—he pushes hard against your forehead—"then a weapon in your hands will only be a danger to yourself and others."

Yes, but if I had a sword, I would set some things right, you think.

True Man reads your thoughts. "What would you set right, right now? With heart and head, if you could change the world, what would you change? Tell me three wrongs you would give your life to change. Three lies you would speak truth to. Three lives you would save. After all, a man must stand for something or he will fall for anything. So tell me, Questor, what would you stand for?"

....

....

....

....

....

....

....

....

....

....

....

....

You continue walking along together. It is cold, and a high wind whistles in the air. You shiver. True Man throws his cloak over your shoulders.

"Not every weapon is made of metal, Questor. I see you carry the Three Lost Scrolls."

Teeth chattering, you can only nod. *Strange*, you think, wondering why you haven't opened them yet. *It just hasn't seemed like the time.*

You walk beside a small stream of melted snow. You bend down and drink. The frigid water is clean and delicious, but so cold you gasp for air. True Man laughs, delighted.

"Takes your breath away, doesn't it? They call this Mount Transformation for a reason. What happens below, what is revealed above—it gets inside you, like a blast of pure truth. When you come to know what you are *made of* and *meant for*, it changes a man forever."

Suddenly, the stream empties over a cliff, spilling into miles of empty air, turning into rain. You stand on a precipice overlooking a steep gorge. In the center, a minaret of rock rises from the mist below. It is enormous but dwarfed by the mountains that surround it—a needle of weathered stone that flattens and expands at the top to a base roughly even with your own height. Eagles soar in the air around the base. A natural stone bridge, only a few inches wide, reaches across the open gulf below from the mountain ledge to the base of the stone needle's platform.

"The Balancing Act," says True Man gravely. "Yonder is Inspiration Tower. Questor, the experiences you've acquired, the transformation of character you've gone through, are meant to be fuel for your future. What did I tell you to remember, at the very beginning?"

You swallow hard. "That I am . . . you said that I am meant for greatness."

"And it is still true. Even with the mistakes you've made. It will be true forever in my plans and heart for you. But to live greatly, a man must take risks. Transformation is not enough. You need vision and inspiration, and those do not come easily. But beware! Below is the River Compromisery. Many piteous lives have drowned below. Ambition is both virtue and vice, depending on how you handle it. Never sell your soul for fame or money or power. Never yield your convictions or ideals on your way to greatness."

True Man waits, studying you. It is as if he is measuring you by how you understand his words.

"A great life is a *meaningful* life," he continues. "Forget this, and you will fall. You will be miserable, despising whatever measure of success you may have achieved, for you will secretly despise yourself. Avoid the lure of shortcuts. Be wary of impulsive decisions. Serve others before thinking of yourself. The one who wishes to be the greatest must be the servant of all. This is the key to *righteous* ambition, and it is a worthy goal. If you lose this balance, you will fall. You will drown. But if you hold yourself steady in the Gorge of Winds, from here to there, you will learn to soar with eagles."

You stare at the flat surface of the bridge. It is barely two foot-widths wide. Wind howls all around you, whipping at your hair.

"There is no other way?"

"There is. But you do not want it."

"It seems so risky. I've been taught not to be stupid."

"You have been taught well. To pursue risk for the sake of thrill is folly. But there are treasures that cannot be won without risk. To pursue meaning and truth . . . to fight, even within yourself, for substance . . . to rise from the ashes of struggle with fresh vision for your life . . . this is not just what a man does. It is *who* a man is. For this, a price must be paid. If you do not pay this price to keep your heart alive, it will shrink to the size of a stone, for that is all it will be."

DAY TWENTY-NINE

YOU GIVE TRUE MAN back his bear-fur cloak.

"I'm not dressed for this place. But I'm afraid this will throw me off-balance in the wind."

Trembling, you place one foot on the rock bridge, test it with your weight. It is firm. You look back sheepishly at True Man. His face is intent, fierce with pleasure, focused on you.

"I am proud of you, Questor. Whether the winds take you or not, I am proud of you. Many never summon the courage to chase their dreams."

His pride makes your heart swell. As you inch forward, you feel as if you are about to cross a line and leave a place to which you may never return. Winds or no, *something* is going to take you from here. Once both feet are firmly planted on the rock bridge, a blast of wind hits you so hard you fear you will be lifted off the rock and swept away. You throw out your arms, steady yourself.

"True Man!" you cry, not daring to look back for fear of losing your balance. "Save me!"

Through the keening wind, you hear a deep, booming voice.

"Questor! Trust your feet. They have been trained more than you realize!"

This strikes you as bizarre and hardly helpful. What you wanted was a hand. Or a parachute. Or a pair of wings.

Even though you know you shouldn't, you peek down past your feet. A gulf of empty air opens below you like a bottomless ocean. You are higher than clouds, higher than birds. Far below, eagles fly. Miles below their wings, you glimpse a ribbon of blue.

The River Compromisery, you assume, reeling. You pull your gaze up again, but your stomach has already landed in your feet. You feel dizzy. Sick with fear. Paralyzed. Wind is tearing at your skin, your legs, your face. You bobble and bend, fighting for balance.

"Nothing is worth this!" you shout back angrily.

"Everyone who turns back says this," True Man bellows. "But none who press on."

You take another faltering step. If you could bend down and clutch the narrow rock with all fours, wrap around it, and never let go, you would. Standing with your feet side by side, each foot overhangs an inch or more on either side. Focusing ahead, on the stone spire in the center of the gorge, your destination, you take a step. And another. Another blast of wind slams against you. Your feet slip. You flail and flap. You are about to fall. You feel yourself careening over the side. Barely above the wind, you hear an echoing voice. A song to die to. Or is it a memory?

Trust your feet. . . .

All at once, you understand. And as you remember—as your feet remember—you catch yourself just before falling. You close your eyes.

Yes, that feels more natural.

That's how the Mines were. Dark. Yes, that's how the stone felt under your feet, heavy with iron, trapped in the Shackles of Discipline. For months, your steps were no bigger, no wider than those cursed chains allowed. Yet in the midst of all that pain, your feet found their rhythm. You learned to walk a tight stance, a narrow pace, a straight line. You learned the slow, steady grind of stone against sole. As the wind blows, you even feel the bite of shackles into your skin.

It feels like a promise that you will, indeed, make it.

True Man is shouting behind. The wind cannot drown out the emotion in his voice. "I love those I discipline," he calls, his voice cracking with pride. "And I discipline those I love. I love you, Questor! You can do this. You have what it takes. Even now you are becoming a man!"

A deep, mysterious sense of calm comes over you. Though the wind rages, you hardly even feel it now. You have been trained.

It is time to soar with eagles.

LET A MAN EXAMINE HIMSELF.

1 CORINTHIANS 11:28 NKJV

DAY THIRTY

SAFELY ACROSS, you step onto the ledge of the center spire, which expands to a broad landing perhaps twenty feet in diameter, covered, amazingly, with the greenest of grass. It is like standing on an island suspended in a sea of air. Though you do not know how or why, the winds have calmed. In fact, the air is perfectly still. The snow has stopped. You don't even want to think about how high up you are. You are thankful for solid ground.

In the center of the platform, you find a simple stone table and behind it a small dogwood tree. Even in the mountain cold, the tree is in full bloom. The table contains several objects, not the least curious of which is a living blue flame, fueled by nothing. It burns from a hole in the center of the table, steady and strong, though you see nothing underneath by which it might be fed. In front of the flame lie a telescope, a whistle, a key. And a new change of clothes. Your old clothes are worn thin, and far too tight, but the new clothes look just your size.

On the other side of the rock bridge, True Man is gone. Again. Your heart sinks.

But you don't have time for sorrow right now. You are cold, and these new clothes look especially warm. In the midst of leather and cloth—boots, britches, gloves, hooded cloak—you glimpse something shimmery and metallic. Under the britches you see it: a long shirt of chain mail, made of ringlets of some sort of white metal. Gasping, you tear off your old clothes, put on the new. They fit perfectly. Especially the chain mail.

Sweet!

You look around for a keyhole but can't find one, so you put the key in your pocket and move over to the telescope. It is huge, elegant, with a shell made of polished ivory. A thin line of instructions has been etched into the surface, but they are written in a language you do not understand. A large button is positioned next to the eyepiece. Timidly, you press it. Internal motors whirr and grind, and the telescope swings into a viewing position, pointed past the clouds and toward a gap between two mountain peaks.

It awaits you.

You look inside. Startled, you jump back, then look again. Sure enough, you see yourself through the telescope. You are standing at the last place you remember before this dream began. You watch, amazed. Slowly, the telescope begins to pan left. As it moves, you see your life in rewind. You go back weeks, then months, then years. All of your memories unfold, but you are watching as another person might have witnessed them, rather than through your own eyes. It is a strange feeling. You see yourself with a detached clarity that you were not able to experience when living those moments. There are good moments. Bad moments. Angry moments. Laughter. Joy. Pain. Disappointment. Impatience. Foolishness. Courage. Sports. Music. Skateboarding and school. Family and friends.

Your life.

As you watch, you recognize with pride and thankfulness a particularly good decision you made once. It is . . .

....

....

....

You also notice a particularly bad decision you made once. Words, actions, thoughts. You feel ashamed to watch, because it seems so clearly wrong now. . . .

....

....

....

REMEMBER THE FORMER THINGS LONG PAST.

ISAIAH 46:9

DAY THIRTY-ONE

WATCHING YOUR LIFE, various odd things strike you. As the telescope continues to scan your history, you are able to zoom in and out, to pause on important moments, to recognize patterns you've missed while living in the midst of it all. You realize, almost for the first time, the involvement of your mom or dad in training and raising you. Was it enough? In the same instant, you feel strangely aware of times when it felt like one or both of them were absent in areas where you truly needed them. . . . Yet it was mostly good. Wasn't it? *Was it good?* you ask yourself. Was it helpful, too stern, too lenient? These are all questions you ponder. As you gaze through the telescope, you can't help but reflect on their love, their words, the time they've spent on you, and other elements of your upbringing. These seem so vivid and clear now. You open your journal and begin to write.

My favorite quality or character trait and how it developed . . .

....

....

....

....

....

....

....

....

My parents' use of discipline and correction . . .

....

....

....

....

....

....

Favorite gifts I've received . . .

....

....

....

....

....

....

Special ways I was provided for . . .

....

....

....

....

....

....

....

Great holiday moments . . .

....

....

....

....

....

....

....

....

Treasured memories with friends . . .

....

....

....

....

....

....

....

....

Good things about my siblings . . .

....

....

....

....

....

....

....

....

> I WILL REMEMBER . . . PONDER
> . . . AND MEDITATE.
>
> PSALM 77:11–12 ESV

DAY THIRTY-TWO

YOU KNOW THERE IS MORE TO PONDER, so you keep writing. This feels like more than merely a review of memories; it feels like an opportunity for inner gratitude to replace inner complaining.

Spiritual and moral guidance that has stuck with me . . .

....

....

....

....

....

....

....

Mistakes I've learned from . . .

....

....

....

....

....

....

....

Other key moments . . .

....

....

....

....

....

....

....

....

....

....

....

....

....

> HONOR YOUR FATHER AND
> YOUR MOTHER . . . THAT IT MAY
> GO WELL WITH YOU.
>
> DEUTERONOMY 5:16 ESV

DAY THIRTY-THREE

MEMORIES KEEP FLOODING IN, faster than you can absorb. You find yourself breathing hard, almost passing out as waves of recognition crash into your heart.

This is my life!

You see the hand of God at work. You see grace and mercy. You see difficulty, strength, and hope.

Then you see your mom and dad. The ones who gave you life.

You see them like you have never seen them before. You cannot help but grow thoughtful.

Qualities I love and respect about my dad . . .

....

....

....

....

....

....

....

....

....

....

....

....

Qualities I love and respect about my mom . . .

....

....

....

....

....

....

....

....

....

....

....

SORROW IN MY HEART.

PSALM 13:2 ESV

DAY THIRTY-FOUR

THE TELESCOPE WHIRRS AND GRINDS AGAIN, but this time the lens doesn't move. In fact, the picture inside has grown dim. The sound is coming from a square-shaped box attached to the bottom. From this box, a sheet of glass the size of notebook paper slides out and hangs there, waiting for you to take it. As you reach for it, it falls to the ground, fracturing into several pieces.

Questions catch in your throat, for the glass is not merely glass. It is a mirror of some sort. You see an image captured in it, like a glass photograph. An image from the telescope, from your past.

It is an image of sorrow. The deepest pain of your young life.

Like the glass, this part of your heart is broken. As you stare at the picture, you begin to weep. You cannot control the tears. They burn hot in your eyes, hot in your soul. This period of your life was *never* supposed to happen. But it did—proof that the world was fallen, pain was real, and hearts could break. For better or worse, this moment changed you, stole something from you. Something you can never get back.

The disappointment and pain are beyond anything else you've ever known. You have struggled to bear the pain, almost wanting to forget it because it hurts so badly. You have been angry. You have been numb. But now . . . now you remember.

Like a knife, the shattered glass punctures this wound of forgotten sorrow. And like an old wound, pus, infection, grief, and sorrow spill out.

For once, there are no right or wrong words, no right or wrong ways to feel or say what you need to say. You feel a clarity of grief and a desire to name it, express it.

How could this have ever happened? How could God have allowed it? How will you recover? You know how you felt then, how you've tried to pretend since, how you've tried to escape the pain. But you cannot escape it. You must go *through* it. And so you write. . . .

He himself will be saved, yet so as through fire.

1 CORINTHIANS 3:15

DAY THIRTY-FIVE

EMOTIONALLY SPENT, you lie for what feels like hours on the thick carpet of grass, feeling the sun shine down on your tear-streaked face. You have cried more than you have in a long time. And in the midst of the bitterness, you have smiled, remembering the good in the midst of the pain. In some respects, this part of the journey has felt harder than anything yet, harder even than the Mines. But facing the awful pain has felt good too. In some strange way, your insides feel scrubbed and clean, though still quite tender. You realize your emotions are sometimes difficult to admit or understand. *Feeling*, for a man, is sometimes hard, because it can so easily feel like weakness. But you know this is not true. In fact, something about tears—something difficult, but necessary—strikes you as vital, *especially* for a man. How can a man experience and display intense emotion without becoming controlled by it?

Knowing this, you are a bit confused. After naming and feeling your grief, and feeling somewhat cleansed and freer, you still carry a *heaviness* you can't define. Climbing to your feet, you wonder what to do next. Absent of a better idea and pricked with curiosity, you take the whistle from the table and blow it. The sound it makes is high and clear and wild, like the cry of an eagle swooping in for the kill. Immediately, a matching cry rises from the empty air below you. In a flash of feathers, an enormous bird rises from the chasm, flutters its wings, perches on the ledge, stares at you. The rush of air from its ascent nearly knocks you over. Its feathers and eyes are piercing blue, like the purest sapphire sky distilled and concentrated to ten times its normal strength.

You feel afraid. Fascinated, but afraid.

"I am the Messenger of God," the great eagle says in a voice that sounds like a gust of autumn wind. His eyes are noble and fierce. His talons, as long as your legs, cut into the rock with the force of steel. "I am the Spirit of Prophecy. The Visioneer. I am the Foresight of Imagination. Do you wish to ride my wings and dream your dreams?"

Trembling, you cannot find words. You can only nod.

"First," says the Visioneer, "you must Fire Wash. You carry guilt. You have witnessed your past. You have visited sorrows beyond your control as well as shames of your own making. Only the pure in heart may truly see reality. Place your hands in the Flame of Unquenchable Mercy. Be brutally honest with yourself. Though the flame will burn, it brings healing to the soul."

You don't know what any of this means, really, but the great eagle continues to stare at you so forcefully you find yourself moving toward the table, toward the flame. You glance hesitantly from blue bird to blue fire. You feel the heat of it.

Never play with fire, you think wryly. *That's what the adults always say.*

But you have come to trust that this process—this whole, strange dream—is ultimately good. Summoning your courage, face scrunched and braced for pain, you thrust your hands into the flame.

The pain is immediate, intense, searing . . . but not physical. Though you nearly jerk away, the flame is magnetic. It holds you in place. You start to shake, to cry out. A door opens within you. The lingering heaviness collapses upon you with suffocating force.

Brutally honest, the Visioneer said. *Sorrows beyond your control . . . shames of your own making . . .*

Fresh from your experiences with the telescope, you discover the great eagle's words trigger more memories. You realize you have not only *been* wronged, but you have wronged *others*. With words, with carelessness, with selfishness, with secret thoughts. You remember how others have done the same to you, in similar ways. And so, on many levels, you realize you have need of forgiveness. It is a fire to face, to feel, but you do not shrink back. As the pain of the flame unlocks the pain of your soul, you confront yourself within the memories, and you make choices. Will you forgive—

"Others?" the eagle says, in sync with the fire. Your eyes are squinted shut with pain, but you hear his airy voice whispering on the wind. "*Whom* will you forgive? And for what? Be specific. . . ."

I ACKNOWLEDGED MY SIN . . .
AND YOU FORGAVE THE GUILT.

PSALM 32:5

DAY THIRTY-SIX

THE FIRE WASH INCREASES in intensity. Though it burns, the pain comes with a sense of release, leaving you feeling cleaner, somehow truer to yourself. Somehow more whole and real, as if you had been trapped under a weight but are no longer, as if you had been hollow and made of straw but now you are flesh and blood. Yet you are not done. The Visioneer speaks again. "And what of your own shame or weakness or failure, Questor? Do you have cause to be guilty within? In what do you blame yourself for false reasons? In what do you feel rightly convicted by God? In either case, can you *forgive yourself* and thus be released? Sometimes this is the hardest of all cleansings. . . ."

....

....

....

....

"Finally, though He has done no wrong against you, it is a fact of your kind that you may hold God guilty in your own thoughts for wrongs you have suffered. Do you blame Him? If so, do not be afraid to admit this. Admitting it will not surprise Him or anger Him. If you do blame Him in any way for any thing, it is the fact of how you feel, and it must be faced. The sweet burn of mercy is for just such broken moments of the soul. Questor, can you forgive God? Will you? Remember, He does not need it. But perhaps you do."

....

....

....

....

....

....

....

....

....

You no longer feel the fire. The burning is complete. You pull your hands out of the flame. They are not burned. Not even a single hair is singed.

Yet you feel alive, free.

DAY THIRTY-SEVEN

"Now it is time to fly!" says the Visioneer, beckoning you with a motion of his head.

You don't hesitate. You leap onto the back of the great bird.

"Clutch my neck feathers!" he cries. "We are going to go high!"

He steps off the side of the platform. Falls. The world spins. You tighten your grip on his thick feathers, gulping for air. You cannot even find a voice to scream. The bottom of the world has dropped beneath you. You are plummeting downward. . . .

Upward.

Effortlessly, the eagle spreads his wings. A mighty updraft of wind catches you, him, lifts you both with jarring force high above the mountaintops. You see the platform dwindle beneath you. All around are clear, cloudless skies, and below is the tiny scale of faraway earth: tiny trees, tiny rivers.

"There are two purposes for vision," says the Visioneer. "The first and easiest is to dream—to think *big*. To imagine possibilities. To recognize and name the passions buried inside your heart so that you can more easily find your place in this world. This is where you say *who you want to be* and *what you want to do* through your teen years and on into full manhood."

You strain to hear the Visioneer over the roar of the wind in your ears.

"Yes!" he cries, as if agreeing with your focus. "Yes, of course, your dreams may change as you grow older. But putting names to desires is important because it focuses you. It is better to start than to stagnate.

Why? There is a proverb: It is easier to steer a moving ship. So, Questor, tell me your dreams. . . ."

....

....

....

....

....

....

....

....

....

....

....

"Good! The second purpose of vision is to gain clarity of soul. To focus your energy so that you can actually *achieve* something, rather than simply talking about achieving. Wishing, but never doing. Many men are dreamers. Great men dream, then *do*. This requires clarity. So here is the more difficult task of vision. What can you do to make your dreams *more* likely to come true? Remember, no one is promised their dream! But the surest way to miss your dream is to think you deserve it without working for it."

You cannot believe how high you have flown. Your stomach lurches. It is thrilling, dazzling, scary. Glorious. It feels as if you can see the whole world from here. Yet the air is thin, and you begin to feel it in your lungs. You realize that at some point you will have to come back down to earth. The Visioneer seems to be leading you to that very place in your thoughts.

"So, Questor, what sacrifices are you willing to make? Yes, even now. You are not too young to begin thinking these things. College? Then what kind of student should you be now to receive scholarships and superior choices? A man of faith? Then how are you feeding your spirit? What series of smaller goals can lead you to the bigger goal? What should you be doing now to prepare for tomorrow?"

DAY THIRTY-EIGHT

AFTER YOU NAME YOUR DREAMS, the Visioneer carries you far and wide, showing you lands and sights you've never imagined. You travel through history, witnessing warriors, conquerors, explorers, adventurers, daring deeds, and noble sacrifice. Cruelty and compassion. Strength and weakness. Freedom and bondage. You see it all. Abraham. Noah. Pharaoh. David. Plato. Socrates. Paul. Justin Martyr. Irenaeus. Genghis Khan. Columbus. Da Vinci. Ponce de León. Galileo. Isaac Newton. George Washington. John Wesley. George Whitefield. Hudson Taylor. Robert E. Lee. Lincoln. Hitler. Stalin. Patton. MacArthur. You see empires form, then fall: Babylon, Egypt, Israel, Maya, Greece, Rome, Germany.

You see yourself standing on the backs of the giants of history, awaiting your turn. In that moment, you realize you should take note in the future of what stories, what heroes, move your soul the most. Very likely they hold keys for your own life as it unfolds.

Slowly, you circle downward, coming to rest by the waters of a placid lake at the base of Mount Transformation. You dismount to find True Man waiting for you. When you turn back to the Visioneer, he has risen up and away and is already small in the distance. You feel overwhelmed with gratitude for your soaring journey together, but also a pang of sadness that you could not tell him good-bye. But you have no time. A booming voice commands your attention.

"With vision comes strength," True Man declares, his words echoing over the water.

He carries a bundle of folded fabric. From this, he withdraws a scabbard. It is polished and finely crafted. It is beautiful.

"When the occasion calls for it, a man must be ready to fight for what is true. For those he loves."

He holds out the sword with the haft facing you.

"Young man, take your weapon," he says with a gentleness that surprises you. "But remember, your enemies are not people. Your enemies are fear, darkness, lies, injustice. Apathy. Pride. These lie within you too. Face what lies within, with honesty, before you go about waving your sword, pretending to fight for a cause."

Gingerly, you place both hands on the haft and pull. The blade slides cleanly free with a cool scrape. It is breathtaking. A strange metal—black as night, razor-sharp.

"Forged from the molten metal of a fallen star," True Man murmurs. "Very rare."

He starts walking. You follow, belting the scabbard around your waist. It feels good.

"A sword is like truth," True Man says. "It cuts, wounds . . . but it also saves. It is a spiritual weapon. Such are all things of the Spirit of God."

The path meanders down into a marshland. The ground softens more and more as you walk on the wet earth and bog grass. Not too far away, a solid footpath leads away to the left and higher ground. In the distance, following this path, you spy a large castle. Colorful banners snap in the wind. A trumpet call rises from the watchtower, sounding like an invitation to feasting.

"Not there," True Man warns solemnly, seeing your wandering gaze. "That place is death to a man's soul. There," he says and points across the swamp, through the muck and mire. You follow his finger, see a little hut on stilts at the far edge of the marsh, then, on a hill, a tree surrounded by laughing people. Beyond that . . .

"I can't see. What are you pointing at?" you ask, annoyed. You already want to go to the castle.

"You will know it when you get there."

His answer irritates you even more. You're getting a little tired of this.

"You know, this may come easy for you, but it's a hard journey for the rest of us," you say. Though you continue to finger the haft and scabbard of your new sword with appreciation, you are also more than a little indignant. "Sure, I've seen amazing things. But it's been harder than I thought. A *lot* harder. I have to constantly guard myself against so many things. Temptation—even a little slipup can cost me big-time. Weariness. Loneliness. I have to work. I have to pick the right friends. I have to persevere. It takes focus. Really, I don't know that I'm ready for manhood. I don't know that I can pull it off."

Somewhat embarrassed by your confession, you look down at your feet, feeling stubborn.

When you look up, it is into the gaping, screaming maw of a monster.

BEHOLD, I AM UNSKILLED.

EXODUS 6:30

DAY THIRTY-NINE

THE BOG MONSTER is a hulking beast of mud and bone, somehow brought horribly to life. It is huge—three times your size, dripping with moss and weeds and stench. It has two arms the size of tree trunks and a face that is mostly mouth filled with sharply chiseled rocks for teeth.

Before you can gather your thoughts, it swings.

You fumble for your sword, duck just in time to avoid being crunched by the massive forearm. The blade won't come free. You aren't used to it. You roll, spring to your knees, mind reeling.

The Bog Monster bellows a sound both high and deep. And deafening. You cover your ears, nearly passing out. Finally, you manage to pull your sword free. Your feet are sinking in muck, making it hard to maneuver, but you do, with effort, trying to climb to higher ground. The Bog Monster is ponderous, but its stride is enormous. You can't move fast enough.

It swings again.

A clawlike branch protruding from the clumpish paw grazes your leg, drawing blood. You cry out in pain, flail wildly at the beast. A lump of something falls off. The beast bleeds green goo that stinks.

It howls again, angry, but not necessarily pained. It may have no feeling whatsoever. It comes at you again, and again. You cannot move fast enough or swing hard enough. It is relentless.

It occurs to you, for the first time in your life, that you could die. Here, in this marsh. With a heart full of terror.

You strike at the beast's leg. Your sword lodges in something like dense clay. You barely pull it free. The Bog Monster swats at you, knocks

124

you twenty feet away. You fly through the air, slam into a pool of water. The beast blows steam and mud into the air, full of blind rage. You can barely breathe. It feels like you might have cracked a rib.

Behind the beast, you spy the path to the castle, its banners snapping in the breeze. Solid ground. No monster. You don't have to fight. You don't have to prove anything. No one will watch you run away. No shame.

By now, fear has gripped your heart. You don't know how to beat this thing. You imagine it is probably unbeatable—foolish to even try.

Wisdom (yes, wisdom!) says you should flee. A man may need to fight sometimes. But he should also know when a battle is lost. Right? A thousand such thoughts flood your mind in two seconds' time. A battle rages, more fierce even than your fight with the beast.

Do I have what it takes? you think. In response to your silent question, you know the answer. You have been given gifts. From the time of your birth.

The things I'm good at, the areas where I feel confident and successful are:

....

....

....

....

....

....

The beast lunges, tries to crush you with his massive arm. You barely dodge. Your mind races.

But there are other things I'm not so great at. I'm usually afraid even to try these things:

125

....

....

....

....

....

....

....

You glimpse the castle again. It looks like a palace, really, all shiny and new and lavish. It is your only hope. You roll away, leap, gain a step . . . and flee.

THE PALACE
OF PLEASURE

THEY HAVE PREPARED A NET FOR MY STEPS.

PSALM 57:6

DAY FORTY

THE WAY TO THE CASTLE IS SHORT, but the Bog Monster has no power on dry, solid ground. He leaves you alone. You try to reassure yourself of the rightness of your decision but are plagued with doubt. A sense of failure nags you. You stand a little taller, puff out your chest, brandish your sword. *It was an amazing fight, eh?* you say to yourself, trying to feel better. Bigger. But your heart knows the truth. How will you ever get across the swamp, where True Man said you must go, without facing the monster?

Before long, you arrive at the castle. The drawbridge is down, and the guards welcome you with smiles.

"Best go straight to the dukes," one guard says politely. "This being their place and all. They're three brothers. They'll have a word for you and plenty of help. Straight ahead, through the big doors. Can't miss it."

Cheered, you follow his advice. Maybe this wasn't such a bad decision after all. Maybe True Man hasn't met the new owners? Feeling smug, you cross the bridge and walk through the big doors and down a long hallway. In a large chamber with plush red carpet, high windows, and higher columns, you find three men reclining at a table, eating their fill, laughing. Sure enough, they are dressed like royalty in fine velvet and gold and leather. They see you enter.

"Well, well! Look at the mud boy, fresh from the swamp!" says a clean, handsome man. "Really, lad, did you have to come straight here? I mean—and please don't take this rudely—but you *stink*!" He laughs coarsely. "And just look at your clothes. How out of style could you be? I suppose if there is one saving grace, it's that the mud helps hide the awful colors underneath. You don't even match. Have you looked in a mirror? Do you even care about your hair?"

Suddenly, you feel very self-conscious. These people are royalty, after all! *Dukes.* You've never met a duke. You should have been more mindful, even though you have no idea where you could have gone to clean up.

In a flash of insight, you realize something. How comfortable are you with your own outward appearance? You think about how you would describe yourself to a blind person:

....

....

....

....

....

....

It occurs to you that God made you a certain way. Do you approve? Is it good or bad in your eyes? What would you keep? What would you change?

....

....

....

....

....

DAY FORTY-ONE

"DON'T YOU MIND VANE," the second man says pleasantly. He is younger than the first man, sharp-eyed. "Vane's always uptight about looks. Although, if you don't mind me saying so, he does have excellent taste . . . and you could use a few good tips. No offense. In fact, now that I think about it, let's bring in some groomers!"

He snaps his fingers. Instantly, four groomers surround you.

"Whoa, hey!" you say, shifting away from their scissors and toenail clippers and measuring tape. "Easy there, fellas. Can we do this later?"

"Ha, sure! Right. I'm getting ahead of myself."

"Pish-posh!" the third duke says, a rotund man with a bulging belly. "You're always ahead. Always more, more, *more* with you. Look at the man. It's clear he's been hard at work. Fighting in the bog, no doubt. Well, good show, lad, but it's just as well you came our way. Battles bring out the worst in men, I think. Get them all bothered about things that can never change and take way too much effort to try." He leaned forward, sweating. "For heaven's sake, boy, am I talking for my health? Sit down and eat. Take a load off your feet."

Another snap of the fingers from the same snapping duke. A trio of stewards come bearing platters of all manner of food—juice, fruits, breads, cheeses, meats, sweets. Enough for ten people.

You stare at it, astonished.

"Not enough?" asks the second duke. Then he bellows, "More!"

Four more platters are hauled in. Foods you've never even heard of.

The fat duke continues, "X.S. is always ready to pile it on, and when it comes to food, I don't argue. He's like that with everything. But all that other stuff can wait. A fellow needs some downtime more than anything—know what I mean? You've got to take care of yourself, prop up your feet. Relax!"

Having finished his sentence and stuffed his face full of food, the third duke promptly falls asleep right where he sits.

"Our manners!" the first duke cries, appalled.

"Yes, shame on us," agrees the second. They rise, bow.

"We are the keepers of this humble abode, and you are welcome here as long as you please," they say. "Our names were carefully chosen by our father, and they have always fit us well."

"I am the Duke of Excess," says the youngest man, the snapper. He looks to be in his late twenties.

"And I am the Duke of Vanity," says the man who first greeted you. His smile is tight with forced politeness. "Really, eat a bite and go bathe. Please. I'll fit you with something decent after. Consider it a gift."

The Duke of Excess waves his brother to silence. Conspiratorially, he points to the sleeping man beside them and whispers, "That's the Duke of Laziness. Forgive him. He's really a charming fellow. Just needs a nap. Every day. Several times."

The Duke of Excess motions for you. "Come, come! I'll show you your chamber." He grins wolfishly. "Trust me, it's huge."

How quickly things can change! you think. Fighting for your life one moment. Perfectly at ease the next.

I could seriously get used to this. . . .

Entranced at your wonderful turn of fortune, you follow the Duke of Excess. You don't care where he takes you. All you know is, following him, you just want *more*.

As you go, you ask yourself, *Is it wrong to want more? Why or why not?*

....

....

....

DAY FORTY-TWO

WEEKS PASS. MONTHS.

You hardly remember the Bog Monster. Even the day you arrived seems lost in the mist that sweeps down every morning from the mountains. The setting of the castle is picture perfect, something out of a tourism ad for Wales or Scotland. Beautiful music wakes you late every morning. You dine like a king. You nap and play whenever you want. The Duke of Excess keeps you endlessly fascinated with his ability to escalate every moment into an unforgettable event. Money is no object. You are lavished with gifts. They tell you this place is called the Palace of Pleasure. And you believe it.

Every morning you wake, look in the mirror, and spend an hour, maybe more, on your appearance. The glass is etched with simple words. They seem deeply true, more so with each day: *Looks matter most.*

Yes, it feels good to look good. You feel handsome, powerful.

But you are not so shallow as all that. Not at all. The larger point is how you have learned style and showmanship. You dress like royalty yourself now, thank you very much.

"Image is power," the Duke of Vanity reminds you. "Nothing should matter more than how you look."

You've taken his advice to heart to the point of being a nervous wreck if every hair is not perfectly in place. But boy, do you look *good*. It's worth it. Everyone thinks you are cool, and that feels good. You are current on fashion and respected for your trendiness. In fact, any visitor who isn't wearing the latest fashion or who doesn't have the right "look," you scoff at. Simpletons. Backward hill people, that's what they are.

An endless series of interesting diversions is ever at your fingertips. You lack for nothing. The Duke of Laziness carves out big chunks of your day for pleasure reading and sipping fresh mango juice.

One day, a woman tears into the castle, screaming, "Please, somebody help! My son is trapped in the bog, and there's a monster gonna kill him."

You take note of the woman's crooked teeth, her torn dress. *Pitiful.*

"Somebody, please!" she cries.

"What? And dirty my new clothes?" you scoff. All the other court attendants laugh with you. Weeping, the woman flees, continuing to cry out for help. Above the laughter of the gathered crowd, her voice stabs your heart, but you can't fathom why. Her request, clearly, was outrageous.

Soon she is forgotten.

The creeping sense of lethargy is not. You feel tired all the time, but never rested. No matter how much you eat, you are still hungry. Even when you are stuffed and sick of food—which is all the time—you are still hungry. No matter how nice your clothes, they all seem plain to you now. When the Duke of Excess shouts for more—of whatever—you roll your eyes. Nothing excites you. Nothing thrills you. Nothing even interests you.

You are bored out of your skull.

This is home now. Life, opulent and privileged. You don't remember True Man, at least not clearly. With each passing day, you remember less and less. All that other stuff was like a dream. A strange, awful dream. Your sword gathers dust. The Three Scrolls are folded up in those embarrassing garments you once called clothes, along with whatever else you took from the top of that mountain. What was it called? The one with the Visioneer. Was that his name?

More time passes. Every day is like every other day. Something about having too much begins to strike you as *not* good. One day, looking out the window of your room, you see something strange. A man is standing in the field, beyond the moat, the drawbridge, the guards. He is facing the castle and holding up a sign. You do not have to squint to read it. The words are big, bold, clear: *"What will it profit a man if he gains the whole world, and forfeits his soul?"*

How strange. He is dressed in rags and has a long beard and fierce eyes. He doesn't smile.

You blink. Look again. Another sign: *"Be on guard against every form of greed; for not even when one has an abundance does his life consist of his possessions."*

You shake your head. *Quite unusual.* The man is planted like a tree and holds a new sign. He doesn't shout. In fact, he doesn't say a word. This sign says, *"What does the LORD require of you but to do justice, love kindness, and to walk humbly with your God?"*

The words burn a hole in your heart. Some part of you that has been asleep for a long time awakens, or at least stirs enough to be puzzled. You know success isn't evil. Nor are fun and games. But what is it about comfort and ease and excess that is so dangerous to the mission God has given man on the earth?

THINGS THAT WILL NOT BE SATISFIED.

PROVERBS 30:15

DAY FORTY-THREE

SINCE SEEING THE MAN WITH THE SIGNS, your life of ease no longer feels so easy. Instead, it's beginning to feel a bit costly, like you might be missing something important. One day, feeling particularly nostalgic or inspired or more bored than usual, you take your old sword—where'd you get it again?—and venture down a long hall made of dark stone. You don't remember having traveled this way before. At the end, you notice a man behind a door made of metal bars. He sits in a tiny room filled with gadgets.

"Hello," you say.

The man glances up. "Wanna see my flamethrower?"

"Umm . . . sure. Whoa! Did you make that thing or buy it?"

With barely a flick of his finger, the man pulls a lever on a tube hooked up to some metal contraption. A thick stream of liquid flame shoots thirty feet past you, singeing your hair. You leap back, crying out. The man giggles with delight.

"Awesome, huh?" He gasps, then looks at you as if seeing you for the first time. "Wait, don't answer. The bigger question is, where'd you get that sword? Good grief, it's ancient. You need a newer model, like *this*!" He pulls out a grand, curving scimitar from underneath a pile of stuff. His sword has gold etching on the haft and a blade polished as shiny as a mirror. "Now, *that's* a sword. And look at this." He pulls a retractable spyglass out of the inner pocket of his robe, hands it to you through the bars. You find a nearby window, gaze out, adjust the focus. It seems like you can see for miles.

"Wow," you say breathlessly. It *is* cool.

"That's nothing. I've got the coolest new stuff. I'm Mr. Gadget. You should want this stuff. It's so cool."

You look around his room. It has nothing but a bed . . . and stuff. Gadgets, gizmos, knickknacks, whirligigs—every conceivable trinket or tool or machine or toy you can imagine. Floor to ceiling.

"Every time something new comes out, I get it. I work and work, and then, whether I have enough money or not, I get it. Why wait? I'm too impatient. All this stuff is so cool." Every time he says "cool," he puts a breathy, dreamy emphasis on the word. On the one hand, it sounds silly. On the other, it's hard to resist.

"Do you ever get out of here?" you say. "You know, outside. Go do something. Play. Have fun." You can't quite locate the word to describe his room—small, stone walls, iron bars—but it seems a strange place to live. What was that called?

Pri . . . pry son? Prison!

Yeah, that's it. Prison. When you're bound up and can't leave.

You were bound up once.

Mr. Gadget looks at you as if you are a fool. "Get out? For evermore . . . *why?*" he asks. Then he shows you the monitors and the padlock. He grips the bars.

"These bars are a rare alloy of tungsten, titanium, and steel, cold-rolled, forming an ultra-high tensile-strength prison. This lock is fashioned with over 113 of the most intricate gears, plungers, and springs, finer than the craftsmanship of any watch. It is unbreakable and foolproof. The monitoring system is state-of-the-art. Any motion by me outside my field creates a wind pattern that flutters into the funnel, releasing a metal ball that rolls down a self-pressurizing tube that shoots the ball the length of the castle, all the way to a gong in the dukes' chamber hall." By now, he is breathless. "It's fabulous. The best prison I could hope for. Except for the Dominator. That's the name of the next upgrade, coming in a couple of months." He crosses his fingers. "I'm so hopeful they'll get it for me."

He studies you. "So . . . what's your excuse for staying here, in the Fortress of Boredom?"

"I'm sorry, what did you call this place?"

"The Fortress of Boredom."

You smirk. "I think you mean the Palace of Pleasure?"

"Nope, wrong. It's a fact. I'm bored stiff. That's why I always need new stuff. I have absolutely zero imagination, and I am utterly addicted to new gadgets. Then, for a few moments, they help me forget my boredom, and I'm happy again. Only then I get bored with the new gadget, and yep—I'm unhappy again. So I need *another* new gadget. On and on. What's your story?"

You don't answer. You hardly hear him. You're still back at two words. *Fortress. Boredom.*

A tinge of recognition, a surge of surprise. Yes, both words seem accurate. You haven't thought of it that way . . . until now. But you feel utterly stuck in boredom.

It occurs to you that if *every* moment is unforgettable, *nothing* is actually memorable.

Life is passing me by. I'm buying it, critiquing it. But I'm not living it. I have everything I want and nothing I need. The adventure is out there . . . and I'm just wasting time in here.

The thought lodges in your gut with a sickening thud. In that moment, you see the Palace of Pleasure with new eyes, as a fortress. Of boredom. For the first time since entering months ago, you see it for what it really is. A small awakening begins in your soul. You ask yourself, *Why is boredom such a huge trap?*

Already you know the answer. . . .

THE DESIRES FOR OTHER THINGS.

MARK 4:19 ESV

DAY FORTY-FOUR

A PRISON. A FORTRESS, designed not to keep people out, but to keep them in.

You hadn't noticed. How could you not have noticed iron bars over every window, every door? Were those there before, or were your eyes just now opened? And the guards everywhere? Why are they scowling at you? You thought, before, they were smiling and pleasant.

You know you've got to escape.

The conversation with Mr. Gadget (such a strange little man!) lingers in your head, trailed by a new thought: *All the gadgets and things I've always liked may actually* cause *more boredom than they prevent!*

This is a revelation. How can this be?

....

....

....

....

....

....

All of a sudden, a sense of urgency compels you. You cannot stay here, not another day. Not even another minute. You rush back to your room, gather everything from the journey thus far. You know how to get out. It seems so clear now. In fact, clarity grows the more you resolve to escape.

You flee down the hallway. A left. A right. Another long hall. You're looking for a particular door, one you've passed a dozen times. Until now, it has made you feel good every time to see what is written above it. Now it sickens you. You want to leave through that door. To make a statement. The symbolism feels important for your soul, a form of repentance.

As you round the corner, two figures emerge from the shadows. They are your age, dressed in black chain mail, black boots, black leather. They are identical twins, with long hair and cool eyes. They carry knives and wear sneers.

You feel fear. "I'm not looking for trouble," you say carefully. "I just want out."

"Out?" says one. His voice drips with sarcasm. "Out of your league, more like. You've never had it so good."

"Dude," says the other. His voice is slow, casual, seemingly unimpressed with everything. "Think with your brain for a minute. Nobody cares what you want out there. Here . . . you can have it all."

"Who are you?"

The twins glance at one another, smug and cunning. With a light flourish, they bow, throw their heads back. "We are the Assassin Twins."

> ## DO NOT CARRY ON AS SCOFFERS, OR YOUR FETTERS WILL BE MADE STRONGER.
>
> ISAIAH 28:22

DAY FORTY-FIVE

"I AM CALLED SCOFFER, AND THAT'S JADE," says the first Assassin Twin, clicking his teeth together, watching you with disdain. "Why the rush, friend? Think for a minute—for once in your life. Add it up. The world is a pretty lousy place, you know. Your parents tell you what to do . . . all the time. Who made them king and queen, right? School bites, bigtime. You almost never get your way, and no one really cares. Am I right?"

You start to answer. Your eyes are on the door behind them, on the words over the door.

It reads, *My Way*.

You remember. Only a few days after arriving at the fortress, you and the Duke of Vanity walked down this hall. He pointed to that door, told you it led to the Myway Highway and, likewise, that the Myway Highway led here. The Pleasure Palace, he had called this place then. Now you know it is the Fortress of Boredom. At the time, you liked the name. After all, here, you were finally getting *your way*.

"I'm going," you say. "You can't keep me here."

"Fine, dude, whatever," says Jade. "I mean, it's like, total whatever. I've been out there too. It has its moments. But . . . been there, done that, got the T-shirt. Who cares? Do you really think it's going to be any better out there than in here?"

"A man should create for others, not merely consume for himself," you say. "Life is bigger than just me. I have been bought with a price. My life is not my own."

"Whatever," Jade repeats, yawning.

Scoffer is more virulent. "You're even dumber than you look," he says haughtily. "Your life is not your own? You only get one life—so who else's is it? Why waste it on anything but yourself? Authority is corrupt. God is nothing but someone's big idea gone bad. You should rebel against both. It would be the first smart thing you've done in a long time. Listen—"

"No, you listen!" you shout, your anger rising. How could you have been so foolish? Waving your arms wildly, as if revealing the whole castle, you say, "Here I'm surrounded by wealth and cleverness all the time. It's unending. So why do I feel poor and bored? If I stay here, I know in my gut I will be surrounded by the illusion of significance but have none of the substance."

"But you will be *free*, dude. To do whatever you want."

You shake your head. "If I'm spoon-fed my freedom from another's hand, am I really free?"

"What is freedom then, if not doing whatever you want?"

Scoffer seems irritated at your answer. "All right, let's cut to the chase. Our job is to keep you here. Mocking and cynicism are our specialties. If you can get up in our brilliant wit and sarcastic attitude, you can be as cool and hip as we are. And you won't want to leave."

"Never let anyone see you care about anything," says Jade. "They'll just take advantage of you."

"Wake up and smell the coffee, kid. A detached, rebellious attitude is *the key* to survival."

"I'm leaving this place," you say more firmly, holding up an object in your hand. "And I have the *real* key."

You took it from Mount Transformation. For a long time, you had forgotten it, hadn't known what it was for. Now you do. Now is the time.

When they see the key, the twins' eyes darken. Howling, they twirl their knives, lunge. Your sword slips free. Stepping sideways, you dodge their thrusts. You counter and backslash. With two swift strokes, you bury your blade in their hearts.

"I will have no part of you," you whisper fiercely.

Gasping, they fall to the ground. As they do, you feel a pang in your own heart, as if they were somehow a part of you, like venom or an infection. Your eyes clear even more. The poison has been sucked out.

You have made your choice. It's time to go.

THE SWAMP

SEEK FIRST HIS KINGDOM.

MATTHEW 6:33

DAY FORTY-SIX

THE KEY IS BIG AND MADE OF WOOD, but hard and heavy like iron. It's shaped like a cross. Carved along the length of it are three words: *Thy Kingdom come.*

Something deep in your core thrills at those three words. It is a thrill unlike any gadget or toy or feast or pleasure you experienced in the Fortress of Boredom. It is better than feeling handsome and powerful. It is a sense of mission, of purpose and significance. You have been born for such a time as this. You have a task, given only to you, by God Himself. The challenge of your life is to find it and fulfill it. You ponder the meaning of all this. How does focusing on the Kingdom of God release you from the boredom caused by worldly enchantment?

....

....

....

....

Enough thinking. You can't wait any longer. Inserting the key, you turn it slowly, holding your breath. It fits perfectly. The door springs open, and light floods in.

For the first time in months, you step outside. Into sunshine. Wind. Fresh air. Green grass. You put the leather strap of the key around your neck. The shape of the cross hangs right over your heart.

Where it belongs . . .

You exit the Myway Highway immediately. Too much time wasted there already. You know where you must go: You must face an old foe.

You start to run, following a side road. As you sprint ahead, you see the old man, the one with the sign. He is holding a new one.

Fear Not, it says.

You don't have time to stop. He gazes at you sternly as you pass by, but there is something solid and reassuring about his eyes. Something familiar. Before long, finally at the edge of the swamp, you take your stand. You unsheath your sword, lean back, and cry out as loud as you can, "Fearful beast, I summon thee!"

And the Bog Monster comes. Rising from the grass and mud nearly a hundred yards away, the beast pulls earth and bone and rock and wood to take his shape, and it is fearsome indeed. He bellows, the sound of a grizzly and a lion and an elephant all rolled into one deafening noise. You feel your knees grow weak. With a few giant strides, he will be upon you.

You have no plan.

Then, a memory.

"Not every weapon is made of metal, Questor."

You drop your sword, fumble through your satchel. There! Veritas, Valorium, Integris.

But which one? Which? The Bog Monster howls in rage, seeing you unmoved. He has cut the distance in half. Some spark of intuition guides you to another memory. This time, you hear your own voice.

"Really, I don't know that I'm ready for manhood. I don't know that I can pull it off."

Today, your battle is fear. Fear of failure. Fear of not measuring up. Of disappointing others. Yourself. Sometimes, the easiest thing for a man to do is not even try, rather than try and fail. You suppose this is because . . .

....

....

....

....

....

....

....

This is a fear common to man. But today, you will face it. You open the Valorium scroll. Inside, it reads,

> *"Not by Might*
> *Nor by Power*
> *But by My Spirit*
> *Says the Lord."*

You don't hesitate. You don't think. You don't question. You seize the moment, the scrap of truth you hold in your hands, and you draw courage from it. The courage to trust. The courage to behave foolishly, if needed.

"God!" you shout. "Deliver me!"

The Bog Monster pauses. Your voice rolls across the swamp only a few feet, then drowns among the fen. Nothing. The sound of marsh birds and mosquitos. Howling again, the beast draws near, his enormous legs pounding, splashing mud. He is almost upon you. You draw your sword, ready for battle. You have asked, trusted. Now you ready yourself. This won't be pretty. But if you must go down, you will give the monster the fight of his life.

One more stride . . .

Out of the corner of your eye, you notice a dark shadow roll across the entire swamp, darkening the sun. Too late, whatever it is. You have no time to think or look. The beast rears back to swing.

And then, it starts to rain.

Pour, really. Buckets of gushing rain come crashing down from the heavens, from a thick pile of clouds that has suddenly moved overhead. Immediately, you are soaked. The beast is soaked. He howls, begins to flail and writhe. His body, made of mud and clay, cannot handle the direct assault of water.

Within moments, he crumbles.

ONE SPIRIT, WITH ONE MIND.

PHILIPPIANS 1:27 ESV

DAY FORTY-SEVEN

YOU MOVE AS SWIFTLY AS YOU CAN through the swamp, heading in the direction True Man told you to follow. The sense of memory, places, and times slowly returns to you. Things forgotten. As you march through the muck and mire, you chide yourself to listen better and trust more. True Man is leading you to a good place, the place you want to go. He knows what he is doing. Stick to your guns and follow and obey. Don't be weak.

Be *true*.

Like him.

As you near the opposite side of the marsh, you approach a shack made of sticks and mud and old wood bound together with ropes, raised on stilts. An old hag is standing on dry ground. She is a map of wrinkles, with beady eyes and a jutting chin and a mole on the tip of her hooked nose with three black hairs growing out of it. She wears black wool and a tall black hat and carries a broom.

"*If* you're going somewhere," she says in a brittle voice that reminds you of sandpaper, "where?"

"To the tree, on that hill." You point. "And then beyond."

"To what?"

"I don't know."

"*For* what?"

"I don't know."

The old hag cackles. Whenever she speaks, she stretches her first word for emphasis. "*If* you don't know—to where, or for what—how will you get there? And why?"

You trudge forward. "Because. I'll just know."

"Oh, you'll know, all right. You'll know if you make one wrong turn and fall off the Rim of Insanity. Or if you get lost in the Forest of Foolishness with a thousand wild pygmies chasing you, thinking you're dinner, or accidentally stir up the Jealousy Hornets and get stung a million times. You'll know if you run headlong into the Black Knight of Pride near Lake Haughty. That's when you'll know. Too late, but you'll know."

None of that sounds good. And of course, you don't know this land. You've narrowly escaped a dozen dangers already. Just left one behind at the other end of this same bog.

"I just want to get to that tree," you say.

"'Course you do! Just listen to old Witch Iff. I'll help you."

"Thank you."

"So you want to go to that tree, but you don't know what for. Well, that makes sense." Her voice drips with sarcasm. "Once you get there, you just want to leave it again, though you haven't quite figured out where to. I see. About as fine a plan as I can imagine. Truly, why bother with details?" She holds a bony finger to her chin, studies you, even though her eyes are white with blindness. She must be ancient.

"I don't really want to just *wander*," you explain unconvincingly.

"Make up your mind. Now you're telling me a different story."

"I am?"

"Which is it?"

"Which what?"

"No . . . *which if*. If you go, where? If you stay, why?"

"Huh? I'm not staying here. I didn't say I was staying."

"Precisely! Which is why you need to stay. Until you know where to go. Otherwise you might arrive nowhere, which is much worse than not arriving somewhere."

The more the old hag talks, the more your brain feels like it's starting to melt. Your thoughts are growing thick like honey. Where are you going? And why? The tree seems like a silly destination if you can't answer a few basic questions. You start to feel dizzy, want to sit down.

"I bet you've made a bunch of mistakes getting even this far," says Witch Iff, clucking her tongue. Confusion thickens in your thoughts.

"Let me fix you some broth. Be a shame to just blunder along farther. That would probably really disappoint True Man."

She pauses, saying the last part cautiously. It is her first and last mistake. The name of True Man shocks you to wakefulness, like cold water in the morning. You close your ears, shake your head, grab the Veritas scroll. Before Witch Iff can speak again, you read aloud,

> "Your ears will hear a word behind you, 'This is the way, walk in it.' . . .
> Only be strong and very courageous; do not turn from it to the right or
> to the left, so that you may have success wherever you go."

It is a simple declaration, but when you look up, Witch Iff has turned to a statue of stone. Her face is contorted in pain. You ponder a deep thought. For a moment, you were starting to feel paralyzed. Past regret and the unknown lay like traps before you. So how does a man balance faith and reason? What does obedience mean when the road is uncertain and you are full of questions?

....

....

You realize that this can be tricky. You remember when you've been stuck in the spell of *if*. *If I had only done it differently. If I hadn't said that stupid thing, I wouldn't have looked like a fool. If only I had tried harder, listened closer, or been a better friend. If only I had more information, I could have made a better choice.* You realize the Witch Iff is a dangerous foe to the soul of a man. If a man can be paralyzed with indecision, he is no longer a force in the world for God's Kingdom. The sorcery of this witch addles the brain, turning men of boldness and action into men of hesitation and self-doubt. Yet wisdom sometimes calls for caution too.

You remember a saying you heard once: "A good plan performed today is better than a perfect plan tomorrow." What do you think about this?

....

....

....

....

....

....

....

....

> He is like a tree planted by streams
> of water . . . its leaf does not wither.
> In all that he does, he prospers.

PSALM 1:3 ESV

DAY FORTY-EIGHT

You leave the bog and the statue of Witch Iff behind and soon approach the hillside with the distant tree. The tree is huge and gorgeous. Its luxurious green leaves, blowing lightly in the breeze, dazzle your eyes. The tree is full of sparkling jewels that twinkle in the sunlight. Or no, you realize, they are actually little pieces of candy.

Other young men and women older and younger than you are climbing the branches of the tree, laughing, stuffing their mouths full of candy. They see you and welcome you.

"Hey! Come on over! You're gonna love this!"

You approach, but your guard is up. After all, you've been down this road before. You think back to the very beginning, when you chose the hard road, the untested road. It's been loaded with difficulties, and almost anything that looked good and easy along the way was loaded with trickery and testing. You suspect this is no different. True Man told you to come here. He did not tell you why.

"Oh man, you gotta try this one," a boy says. He's grinning from ear to ear, holding out a yellow piece of candy just plucked from the tree. "This one is delicious. You'll feel like you're sipping lemonade on a warm summer day. I get a high every time I take a bite."

You hesitate. Should you take it? It does *look* delicious. But still . . . you can't help but feel the irony of your question, since part of what you learned at Witch Iff's was of the danger of getting trapped in questions and doubts that have no answer. But you suspect there is an answer here.

"Does True Man permit us to eat from this tree?"

The boy smirks. "Dude, relax. True Man probably doesn't even care. Besides, everybody's doing it. Look at us. All the cool people come here to eat."

He's right. You hadn't really noticed before, but they do look like the cool crowd. Cool haircuts, cool clothes. They all have that "cool" attitude. As one, they turn to stare at you. You feel the pressure of their gazes. They are measuring you to see if *you* qualify as cool. The jury is out. You can tell that you are expected to perform a certain way if you are going to make the cut. The boy before you is still smiling, friendly-like, but his eyes slightly narrow in judgment, as if to say, "This is your one chance, buddy. Are you good enough to join us?"

"What is your name?" you ask. You try not to notice the others, but you feel their eyes on you. You hear snickering. Your heart starts to pound. The candy must be good. Otherwise, why are they all eating it?

Maybe just one bite . . .

"My name?" The boy repeats your question, acting mildly shocked. "What's it matter? Do you want the candy or not? I'm giving you a gift." He extends his arm once more.

Just one . . .

"Names have meaning," you say. "Your name will probably tell me something about your true nature. I don't trust you yet."

You are surprised at your own boldness. But it's not easy. Instantly, you feel the collective gaze of all the other kids grow hard. They begin to mock.

"Loser! I knew he was a loser," one says.

"Yeah, what a jerk!" says another.

"We were only trying to be nice and look what we get. What a stuck-up."

The boy with the candy speaks up. His face is a challenge. "He's not stuck up . . . he's chicken!"

Everyone around the tree grows silent. A very pretty girl walks up to you. Her eyes are condescending. She tosses her beautiful hair.

"You'll never get a pretty girlfriend like me," she says sweetly, "unless you eat the candy."

After her, an older boy approaches. He looks maybe sixteen. In fact, he looks a lot like one of the popular guys back home—someone you wish you could hang out with, be friends with.

"Look, man, if you're too scared to hang with us, you need to leave. We don't like sissies."

Your own thoughts begin to echo in your head. *Just one bite. It's just* one *bite.*

You feel an intense pressure to give in, be a part. You begin to breathe faster, and your hands grow damp. These are the cool kids! You could join the crowd. Besides, it's only *one time*. . . .

A bird flies overhead. It is a white bird. You have no idea why, but it can speak. It cries out.

"Sustain your life!"

You've heard that phrase before. Where?

"What is . . . your name?" you say again, less confidently. "I need to know."

The boy with the candy lowers his arm. He is no longer smiling. But it seems as if he can't resist. "My *name* is Hollow. Big deal."

You ponder the name, unsure what it means. You don't even notice that the assembly of teens now begins to surround you. They are making threatening gestures, slapping their fists in their palms. For the first time, you are afraid. There are a lot of them.

Then you remember. *Sustain your life.* The note with the Three Lost Scrolls. You have one left.

The crowd looks intense. You can't escape. You grab the scroll, fumble to unroll it, and read aloud:

"We have renounced secret and shameful ways; we do not use deception. Vindicate me, O LORD, for I have walked in my integrity."

Immediately, a wind begins to blow. It blows stronger and stronger. You look around. All the cool kids begin to struggle in the wind. You feel the force of the wind, but it is easy to stand firm. Not so for them. As they begin to twist and turn, you notice for the first time that they are paper-thin. They are shells of paper, shaped like people, but they are empty on the inside. They have no inward substance to support them. They begin to cry out. The wind grows stronger. You hold your ground, while they are blown away.

Stunned, you pull out your journal. You don't want to lose this moment. What made them hollow? Why did they lack substance?

"Young man, I say to you, arise."

LUKE 7:14

DAY FORTY-NINE

You stumble away from the tree, only to find True Man waiting for you on the next hill, overlooking a broad plain. He is beaming with pride. His long hair catches in the breeze, and his eyes look like fire.

"You did well, my son!" he says, pulling you to his chest in a fierce embrace. He kisses your forehead, and you feel the bristles of his whiskers like sandpaper on your cheek. You feel strong in his arms. Strong and safe.

"I didn't trust them. I don't know why, but I didn't trust any of them."

"The Tree of Forbidden Sweets is a difficult challenge to be sure. Most young men fall prey. It is in your nature to want to belong, to prove yourself, to be included. But you must always ask yourself, 'What am I proving? And is this worth belonging to?'"

You nod, telling yourself to remember those questions.

True Man says, "I know that you have faced this test before. You have felt pressure from others to do the wrong thing. If you know something is wrong, why do you think it is hard to stand your ground when others are pressuring you?"

....

....

....

True Man nods at your response. "Good, Questor. It is not wrong to be tempted, only to yield. What people and sources of guidance are in your life that you know you can trust? What things count as *good pressure?*"

....

....

....

....

....

....

....

....

....

....

....

....

DAY FIFTY

AFTER YOU FINISH, True Man puts his arm around your shoulders, and you begin to walk along the ridge of the hill. You remember when you first saw True Man. He was large, fierce, strong, and terrifying. He remains all of those things, yet you are no longer afraid. His strength is for your protection, for your good.

He is on my side, you realize.

He begins to speak, grabbing your attention. "Your voice has deepened over this journey," he says.

Embarrassed, you duck your eyes. The sun is behind you, warm on your back, casting your shadows on the grass and stones ahead of you. You walk for a while, with True Man's arm around you. Neither of you speak. At length, you notice your two shadows. Though a bit smaller, yours is not as small as you thought compared to True Man's. Even more interesting, the way you walk—the measure of your stride, the shifting of your weight—resembles the way he walks. You are pleased.

"Yes, you are becoming more like me."

"Good, because you are the *True* Man."

You know this for a fact, deep in your knower. True Man is not just a title or a name. It is the *reality of who he is*. He is complete in every way: goodness, strength, wisdom, power, servanthood. This man is everything you aspire to be. Almost for the first time, you realize that there is a man in your life, given by God to watch over you, who also

reminds you of True Man, and that he has also set an example for
you to follow. A wave of thankfulness washes over you, mixed with a
little bit of shame. You resolve to honor your father more in the future, knowing that is a major key to a good, blessed life. Regardless,
you consider it a privilege to be trained by True Man personally. Your
voice is deepening; your walk is becoming like his. The thought pleases
you.

True Man stops. His gaze drifts toward the bottom of the hill. You
follow his eyes and see a series of shifting scenes. A city full of people.
A school full of kids grasping at a young man, pulling him in different
directions. You feel the pull within yourself. You see a graduation ceremony, black robes and caps. You see a young man with his nose buried
in a stack of books at the library. You see a beautiful young woman,
smiling. A home with a couple and their firstborn child. The husband
looks like you, only older. You look closer. You are beginning to realize
this is a preview of your life, played out in panoramic vision before you.
You see a vast wheat field and a father and son arriving to harvest the
wheat. Again, you recognize yourself. You are dressed and ready for the
labor, wearing gloves and boots. You look both determined and joyful.
You see many different scenes, one after another. A hospital room. A
day at the park, playing catch. A homeless man, lying on the street,
reaching out to you. A moment of temptation at work with a beautiful
woman who is not your wife. A crisis of faith. A moment of prayer. A
calling, a destiny. You see yourself standing in a storm when the rains
come. You are battered but do not fall, for your feet are planted firmly
on solid rock. Scene after scene, too many to count, tumble along in
front of you.

"Now look again," says True Man. You obey. From the beginning,
every scene begins to repeat. Only now the city is a battlefield. Only
now, in every scene, you are a warrior, wielding your black sword to
defend the weak, guard the innocent, and stab temptation in the heart
when it rises against you. Your sword becomes a scythe in the wheat
field, harvesting the grain. It becomes a beam of light when you kneel
in prayer. It becomes a rock under your feet when the storm comes. It
becomes a musical instrument by which you shout praise to God and

defy the world's small pleasures. Your sword is sharp, clean, and deadly, but it radiates life to your entire being.

"Your whole life is waiting. You are prepared now, but you must be vigilant. Life is joy and pleasure. It is a gift I give. But it is also a battle. Do not be fooled or become careless. If you are born male, you are meant for this challenge. You are meant for adventure . . . and *everything* is adventure—good times and bad. You are meant to be strong. A true man will let others feel the weight of who he is without apology, though humbly." He pauses. "Let me say it another way. A man must stand for something, or he will fall for anything. Tell me what this means to you."

"Well said," True Man responds. "Now, take out your sword and look at it."

Again, you obey. The sword is flawless. Its edges are razor-sharp. It is heavy, but perfectly balanced in your hand.

"You have what you need in that sword, but you need to gain more skill in using it. The sword is a living weapon. It will serve you well. But you must practice handling it *before* you need it. If you wait until you are tested, it will be too late. Do you understand?"

You nod. You feel a surge of excitement rising in your gut. You don't know why.

"Tell me, Questor. What is the sword?"

"It is your Word. It is the weapon of the Spirit of God," you boldly proclaim.

True Man beams with pride once more, and you nearly melt under the pleasure of his gaze. "I will always be with you. For the rest of your life, you will learn from me. You will make mistakes. I alone am the True Man. But if you will continue to follow my path, your reward will be great. Are you ready?"

You clench your sword. You are nearly trembling with anticipation. "*I am ready!*" you cry.

Smiling, True Man points to the grassy field below. The city. The home. The battle awaits.

"Go!" he says.

Every muscle in your body tenses. You turn to face him. Tears stream down your cheeks, even though you are grinning from ear to ear. "Thank you," you whisper. "For everything."

He nods. You linger, not wanting to leave, yet something greater than nostalgia seizes you. It is the call of destiny. You take a deep breath, almost soaring again like you did with the Visioneer. In your imagination, from high above, you see the speck of your own frame below, as if you are outside your own body. Then, from high above, your awareness zooms downward until you slam into yourself—breath and bones, heart and soul, mind and will. You have a story to live, a person to become. A man to be. You have never felt more alive.

There is no time to waste. You begin to run.

"This is your life!" True Man calls behind you. "Live it well!"

His voice overtakes you midstride, propelling you farther, faster. Like a crashing wave striking a rocky shore, the force of it explodes inside you. You run harder, ready for manhood. You leap . . .

. . . feel a strange sensation. Your skin begins to tingle.

Everything inside collapses into a sudden burst of light. As suddenly as it started, the dream ends. The same strange music that marked the beginning of your journey echoes inside your brain, slowly fading away. Startled, you find yourself lying in your bed, alone.

This is my life, you realize. *This is* my *life!*

You rise from the bed, fully awake.

A new day has begun.

Dean Briggs is happily married to Jeanie, is the proud father of eight grown children, and is a grandfather of five. A New Covenant storyteller, Dean loves the magical power of words. He dreams, prophesies, and prays across the world, speaking and preaching on the great story of God. His acclaimed five-part young adult fantasy series, THE LEGENDS OF KARAC TOR, offers Christian families a powerful storyline for raising up champions. A new novel, *The Withering Tree*, is soon to be released. Learn more at deanbriggs.com.

More from Dean Briggs

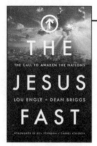

Casting a dynamic vision of how we can turn the tide of evil in our lands, Lou Engle and Dean Briggs reveal that 40 days of prayer and fasting always precede breakthrough, revelations of God's glory, breakage of demonic hindrances and more. Together, through fasting and intercession—using Jesus as our model—we can awaken the nations to global revival and transformation.

The Jesus Fast by Lou Engle and Dean Briggs